Published by  in association with

Pedigree Books Limited, Beech Hill House, Walnut Gardens, Exeter, Devon EX4 4DH

Yours – the leading magazine for women over 50. Look out for it in your local newsagent.
Yours, Bretton Court, Bretton, Peterborough PE3 8DZ. Tel: 01733 264666

Your Good Health: Please consult your doctor if you are unsure about taking any medication
recommended in our health section, especially if you are already on medication.

Thanks to: Charlotte Haigh, Gareth Salter and Louisa Chadderton
Foulsham Publishing for permission to use extracts from Correct Conduct.

*Compiled and edited by Caroline Chadderton, designed by David Reid. Sub-edited by Christine Curtis.
Additional writing by Marion Clark and Bridget Davidson; recipe compilation by Katy Lamb.
And special thanks to all the readers who, as ever, have contributed so magnificently to this Year Book
by sending in their memories, photographs, stories and tips*

£6.99

Hello!

Welcome to the fifth edition of A Year with **Yours** – and I can honestly say it's our best one yet. It's a handy calendar plus a week-by-week collection of tips, memories and bite-sized nuggets of information for you to dip in and out of at your leisure. As always, it is based on your contributions – thank you all so much for your marvellous response – your memories have made us laugh and cry in equal measure.

The Year Book is a culmination of the hard work of a few team members, and masterminded by Associate Editor, Caroline Chadderton. So I'd just like to wish you all the very best for 2006, and hand you over to Caroline.

Best wishes,

Valery

Valery McConnell
Editor, **Yours**

It's a great privilege to have put together A Year with **Yours** 2006 because it's you, the reader, which makes it so special. We asked you for your memories and, as usual, hundreds of letters flooded in. Heartfelt thanks to you all.

Thanks, too, go to the **Yours** team members who have helped with this mammoth task – Bridget Davidson, Marion Clarke and Katy Lamb for help with writing; designer David Reid and sub-editor Christine Curtis. We didn't argue once!

Happy reading during 2006.

Caroline

Caroline Chadderton
Associate Editor (Features), **Yours**

January 2006

Sunday

1

New Year's Day Bank Holiday

Monday

2

Bank Holiday (Scotland)

Tuesday

3

Wednesday

4

Yours January 4, 2006 on sale

Thursday

5

Friday

6

Epiphany, London International Boat Show starts

Saturday

7

Sunday

8

Monday

9

Tuesday

10

Wednesday

11

Thursday

12

Friday

13

Saturday

14

Sunday

15

Monday

16

Tuesday

17

Wednesday

18

Thursday

19

Friday

20

Saturday

21

Sunday

22

Monday **23**	Saturday **28**
Tuesday **24**	Sunday **29** — Chinese New Year
Wednesday **25** — Burns' Night	Monday **30**
Thursday **26**	Tuesday **31**
Friday **27** — Holocaust Memorial Day	

Flavour of the month

Hibernating animals have the right idea! January is the perfect month to slow down and recharge our batteries. After the excitement of Christmas and the New Year, it is a positive treat to stay indoors in the warm, viewing the world from the comfort of a favourite armchair.

While the snow whirls down beyond our windows, we can take the opportunity to catch up on tasks we don't find time for in the warmer months. How about sorting out that drawer full of photos, for starters? Even if you don't put them all in albums, it is a good idea to write a few details on the back of each snap – where it was taken and the date, for example.

Even dedicated gardeners don't venture out at this time of the year. Instead they happily pass the time poring over seed catalogues, planning colourful summer borders and bountiful vegetable patches. The only occupants of the garden are the birds, gratefully pecking away at the seeds and peanuts. Without leaving your armchair, you can take part in the RSPB's Big Garden Birdwatch by keeping a tally of all the different birds that come into your garden during one hour on either 28 or 29 January. For more details, visit website **www.rspb.org.uk/birdwatch.**

If you do feel the urge to be out and about – and still have some money in the bank after buying all your Christmas presents – then take a trip to the January sales. Joining the scrum of shoppers is sure to get your adrenalin flowing and there is nothing like a bargain to give you a real warm glow.

PIC: RSPCA / MIKE LANE

My Mum

My Mother was less than five feet tall, but what she lacked in height she made up for in other ways. She was the most loving and caring person I've ever known.

With four growing, boisterous children, no electricity, no gas, no hot water, no bathroom, and an outside toilet – life was very hard but Mother just got on with things and everywhere was warm and

Tess and her mother

comfortable.

Looking back, my childhood was a very happy one, and I now realise it was all due to Mother. I loved her so very much, but I think she knew that.

Mrs Tess Rawcliffe, St Bees, Cumbria

+YOUR GOOD HEALTH+

Beat the post-Christmas blues

The week after the festive season can leave you feeling as flat and droopy as those limp decorations. Perk your mood up with 5-HTP, a substance your brain uses to make the neurotransmitter serotonin, which controls mood. It's found in oats, fish, turkey and eggs, or you could try taking a 300mg 5-HTP supplement daily (from your health food store) – studies suggest it's more effective than prescription antidepressants for boosting your mood. But if you're already on medication, check with your doctor.

And another thing...

'Let us have wine and women, mirth and laughter, Sermons and soda-water the day after.'
Don Juan

A treasured memento

My dear late Mum was always knitting, especially toys, and she gave me a small knitted panda – Sue – just before she died. Sue brings back so many memories of Mum running along the beach and exploring the rock pools with the grandchildren.

My other treasured memento was a memo pad given to me by my dear and only sister, Betty, the Christmas before she died.

On the first page she'd written:
New Year's resolutions for 1981.
1 Up at 6am. Take Eric a cup of tea.
2 Start looking your age (give your sister a chance!)
3 Have a holiday abroad with your husband.
4 Don't get into panics.
5 Be Happy.

Mrs Dorothy Pomroy, Salisbury

Above: Dorothy and granddaughter Danica with Sue the panda
Below: Dorothy's mum doing what she loved best – knitting

Etiquette for Everybody

– 1920s' style –

On borrowing...
'Some people are habitual borrowers; they will borrow money, clothes, umbrellas, music and a host of other things. Beware of such people, for they will make you poorer in the end.'

A RECIPE FOR YOU

Mustard and Herb Rubbed Leg of Lamb
(Serves 4-6)

- 1 kg (2.2 lb) lean leg of lamb
- 60 ml (4 tablespoons) wholegrain mustard
- 60 ml (4 tablespoons) English mustard
- 2 big garlic cloves, peeled and finely chopped
- 4 sprigs fresh rosemary
- 6 sprigs fresh thyme leaves
- 30 ml (2 tablespoons) olive oil
- 700 - 900 g (1½-2 lbs) potatoes, peeled
- 3 large carrots, peeled, halved, and cut in four lengthways
- 2 red peppers, cored, deseeded and cut into large chunks

1 Preheat oven to 180-190°C, 350-375°F, Gas Mark 4-5.
2 Using a sharp knife make deep incisions all over the lamb joint. Mix together the wholegrain and English mustard with the garlic cloves, and rosemary and thyme leaves. Rub over the lamb and season. If time allows, cover and leave in a refrigerator for at least 30 minutes.
3 Place the joint in a large roasting tray and drizzle with the olive oil. Roast uncovered for 25 minutes per 450 g (1 lb) plus 25 minutes for medium, or 30 minutes per 450 g (1 lb) plus 30 minutes for well-done.
4 Roughly chop the potatoes, carrots, and peppers with 3-4 extra thyme sprigs. Add to the lamb 60 minutes before the end of the cooking time, coat in the lamb juices and roast. Serve the lamb whole or sliced with the vegetables.

- If you wish, cut down on the amount of mustard, to taste

RECIPE COURTESY ENGLISH BEEF AND LAMB EXECUTIVE

Plant of the week

Look out for amaryllis bulbs at your garden centre – many may be cheaper after Christmas and they're worth every penny. These perennial bulbs from the lush river banks of Brazil, Peru and Chile, are simple to grow and will reward you with flowers up to 25cm (10in) in diameter in a vibrant range of colours – white, pink, red, orange and yellow. Their height may vary but their stems can reach 90cm (3ft).

My Prayer

This prayer is my New Year's resolution.
*Let me take time out to listen to You
With rest from work to talk to You
May I always think of You
Each and every day
Help me to keep faith in You
To always put my trust in You
Let me continue to walk with You
All along life's way*
Dilys Parry, Liverpool

TOP TIP

A tip to keep the fizz in a plastic bottle of pop is to give the bottle a few shakes after use, until the bottle feels hard.
Mrs S Hodkinson, Newport

January 9-15

TOP TIP

For removal of stubborn wallpaper use a mixture of water, washing-up liquid and wallpaper paste. The paste will hold the water in place while the detergent speeds up the wetting process.

A treasured memento

Barbara today with two of her daughters

My late husband spent five-and-a-half years in the RAF during the Second World War. When he was demobbed from Hamburg in December 1945, he had a little extra cash, so he left it for flowers to be sent to me for our fifth wedding anniversary, in January 1946.

They were red tulips, which I had every wedding anniversary after that. Last year my daughter bought them for me, some to place where my husband's ashes are buried, and some for me at home. I have always treasured the card my husband sent with those first flowers in 1946, which read, 'To the future and us. Love, Ken.'

Mrs Barbara Elliott, Banbury

And another thing...

'All I need to make a comedy is a park, a policeman and a pretty girl.'   *Charlie Chaplin (1889-1977)*

Plant of the week

Take stock of your houseplants now while there's not much happening outside. Varieties of Ficus benjamina, the fig family, make decorative specimens whether they have plain green or variegated leaves and are useful as a year-round backdrop to other flowering plants. Ensure the compost is always moist but don't overwater, and keep the plants in a warm room away from draughts, direct sunlight and radiators. Diffuse sunlight through net curtains is ideal. They can easily reach 1.8m (6ft) if looked after.
● **Tip** – If you're buying these plants during winter, wrap them up as you walk between the shop and the car as chilly weather can cause leaf loss.

Etiquette for Everybody
– 1920s' style –

On correct dress...
'In winter-time men must not enter the drawing-room wearing their overcoats, and should leave such things as sticks, umbrellas, hats, etc in the hall.'

Marmalade Crumble Cake

- 200 g (7 oz) butter
- 200 g (7 oz) golden granulated sugar
- 1 egg, beaten
- Grated zest of 1 unwaxed orange
- 500 g (1 lb 2 oz) plain flour
- 1 teaspoon baking powder
- 1 jar (450 g approx) Seville Orange marmalade
- Juice of half an orange
- 50 g (2 oz) ground almonds

1 Preheat the oven to 200° C, 400° F or Gas Mark 6.
2 Cream the butter and golden granulated sugar until soft and light, and then stir in the egg and orange zest.
3 Sift in the flour and baking powder and using your fingers, work the mixture until crumbly.
4 Press half the mixture onto the base of a buttered 25 cm (10 inch) round spring-form cake tin.
5 Combine the orange juice with the marmalade and spread evenly over the cake base.
6 Add the almonds to the remaining mixture and spoon over the top, to cover the marmalade.
7 Bake for 40-60 minutes until browned.
8 Cool in the tin for a few minutes, then remove from the tin and leave to become cold on a wire rack.

RECIPE COURTESY BILLINGTON'S

Memories of childhood

I was raised by my maternal grandmother in Liverpool. She was a dressmaker and my most vivid memory of her was fitting a wedding dress, a tape measure hanging from her neck and pins protruding from her lips.

I remember smells of bottled fruit and bubbling homemade jam, of freshly baked bread wafting through the house. I can still taste the rabbit stew, the skin off the top of the rice pudding dusted with nutmeg and the browned potatoes topping a lamb hotpot.

The sounds of gran's treadle sewing machine and music hall songs would lull me to sleep, and I would wake to the rumbling and knocking of the water tank next to my attic bedroom.

A mantelpiece clock ticked loudly in the parlour, and I loved the annual sound of falling soot in the chimney, aided by the sweep's large brush.

I prefer the era when children made theatres, masks and dressed dolls from cardboard cutouts on the back of cereal packets, or who shrieked with laughter while playing Happy Families or Snap.

Doreen McColl, Liverpool

✚YOUR GOOD HEALTH✚

Boost your digestion

Too much rich food and wine through December might have left you with sluggish bowels and constipation. Get things moving by taking three teaspoons of psyllium husks in water 15 minutes before breakfast, and swap your usual cuppa for nettle tea, which encourages elimination. Up your intake of fibre to push waste through your body – oats, brown rice and fruit and veg are excellent sources.

A RECIPE FOR YOU

Dynamite
(Makes 12)

- 12 slices of white or wholemeal bread from a medium-cut large loaf
- 75 g (3 oz) butter, softened
- 3-4 tablespoons tomato pickle or a little Marmite
- 175 g (6 oz) Cheddar or Red Leicester cheese, grated
- 12 rashers streaky bacon
- Cocktail sticks

1 Preheat oven to 200°C, 400°F, Gas Mark 6.
2 Using a sharp knife, and working on a chopping board, cut the crusts off each slice of bread. Flatten the slices of bread with a rolling pin, then spread them with butter.
3 Flip the slices of bread over and spread the unbuttered side with tomato pickle or Marmite. Sprinkle with an equal amount of grated cheese.
4 Lay one rasher of bacon down the middle of each slice of bread, so that it trails of the edge to make a 'fuse'. Roll up the slices neatly and secure them with cocktail sticks. Arrange them on a greased baking sheet.
5 Bake in the oven for about 10-12 minutes until golden brown. Let them cool for a few minutes, remove the cocktail sticks and serve.

RECIPE COURTESY THE DAIRY COUNCIL

TOP TIP

When you're recycling cans, squash them so they take up less room – and wash out food cans first.

Etiquette for Everybody
– 1920s' style –

On conversation...
'Some people are brilliant conversationalists, others, equally intelligent, make a poor show. If you are one of the latter, try to learn from the former. Fluent talking is an art which can be acquired.'

My Prayer

I was unwell while I was on holiday in Tenerife and after my return home, I wrote this prayer.
Here is an extract of Pat's prayer:

A Prayer to Heaven
High on a mountain I will survey
And know my God to whom I pray
Instead of asking questions, 'why?'
When troubles come and pass me by
And when I err and start to stumble
Thinking that my world will crumble
I'll thank you for the days when You
Comforted me and brought me through.
Me – who was made from the dust
Who must learn of God and how to trust.

Pat Melbourn, Poole

✚YOUR GOOD HEALTH✚

Hands on

Most of us don't give our hands a second thought, but they can be one of the first areas to be affected by arthritis and stiffness as we age. Keep them flexible with some simple exercises. Bend the back of each hand towards your shoulders, to stretch the tendons in the wrists. Then splay your fingers out and crunch them into your palm, repeating ten times on each hand. Do these exercises several times a day, while you're watching TV or listening to the radio.

Plant of the week

The vibrant carpet of flowers of Cyclamen coum is a joyful sight during late January. The dainty blooms range between white, pale sherbert and eye-popping cerise. The leaves are also attractive, with silver marbling across the surface. The plants enjoy partial or deep shade and will cope with most soil types as long as they're not waterlogged. H8cm (3in).

● **Tip** – Mulch annually with leaf mould because this will help prevent the tubers from drying out in the summer.

A treasured memento

My most treasured memento is a signed ornamental wooden fan. My husband Peter and I are keen ballroom and Latin dancers, and over the years we've seen many world ballroom and Latin demonstrations danced by world champions.

Hazel and husband Peter

Each time I managed to get signatures from them – the first in 1971, and the last when the fan was full in 1985.

Although we are in our late 70s, we still go dancing and still see demonstrations. The style of dancing has changed over the last 30 years but I still prefer the dancing of the former years. When I look at my fan, I still remember all those wonderful times.

Mrs Hazel Buckland,
Clacton-on-Sea

And another thing...

'There are few hours in life more agreeable than the hour dedicated to the ceremony known as afternoon tea.'
Henry James

My Mum

From when I was small my Mum taught me to sew and make my own clothes. As I grew up, pre-holiday times were a hive of activity, getting all my new things ready on time – it was so exciting. I shall always be grateful to my Mum who learnt it from her mother.

Miss June V Bishop,
Romford, Essex

June's Mum enjoying the sunshine

✚ YOUR GOOD HEALTH ✚

The write stuff

Get scribbling! Writing can help relieve stress and depression, and some studies have even found jotting down your thoughts can ease high blood pressure and arthritis. Keeping a daily diary is a good way to start, or try your hand at getting creative with poems or short stories. Don't feel you should show your efforts to anyone – you'll get the most stress-busting benefits without having any pressure on you.

TOP TIP

On opening a new bottle of oil for cooking, slip the bottle into a plastic bag and it won't make sticky marks on the shelf.

Janet Henderson, Chertsey, Surrey

A treasured memento

I was 11 years old and Ken was 14 when we first met. Ken used to go abroad on school trips and on one occasion he brought me back a penknife which was two inches long in the shape of a lady's shoe and covered in Mother-of-pearl.

Above: Ken aged 15 and Beryl aged 12
Left: Beryl today

Then the war came and Ken joined the RAF and became a pilot. I was 17 and Ken was 20 when he was killed, and so the knife became my most treasured memento.

Mrs Beryl Perkins,
High Wycombe

A RECIPE FOR YOU

Dusted Chocolate Brownies
(Makes 9)

- 150 g (5 oz) plain chocolate
- 100 g (4 oz) unsalted butter
- 2 tablespoons Lyle's Golden Syrup
- 2 large eggs, beaten
- Few drops vanilla extract
- 100 g (4 oz) self-raising flour
- 150 g (5 oz) icing sugar, plus extra for dusting
- 25 g (1 oz) cocoa powder
- 50 g (2 oz) milk or white chocolate chips

1 Preheat the oven to 180°C, 350° F, Gas Mark 4. Break the chocolate into a small pan and add the butter and syrup. Heat gently, stirring until melted; leave to cool slightly.
2 Stir in the eggs, vanilla extract, flour, icing sugar, cocoa powder and chocolate chips, mixing until well blended. Pour the mixture into a 6 in square tin and bake for 25 minutes until set and crusty.
3 Cut into squares and transfer to a wire rack to cool. Dust with icing sugar and serve.

- **TIP:** Try serving these brownies hot from the tin with a scoop of vanilla ice cream or drizzle of cream for a brilliant pudding.

RECIPE COURTESY TATE & LYLE

Lost in the snow

I was ten in 1947, and that winter was never to be forgotten. One night late in January, the living room fire started to smoke, and by bedtime it was billowing down the chimney. Granddad said it was a sure sign that it was going to snow and he was right!

When we looked through the window the next morning, we couldn't see the front gate, or the hedges. My brother Edward and I whooped with delight as we raced down the stairs. We made tunnels through the snow and Edward made a pair of skis, and actually walked over the hedges, which I thought was incredibly clever!

Father didn't have such a happy time, though – he had some cows which were across a couple of fields. He had to make a sledge, which must have been terribly hard to pull, with milk churns on with water for the cows.

Edward and I ploughed down into town with the sledge for some groceries and

Joyce and her brother Edward in warmer times!

once, we lost a ration book and mother was very cross. We had to go back and look for it – luckily, someone had handed it in at the bakers.

It snowed, on and off, for four weeks and lasted for about nine weeks but eventually the thaw set in, much to everyone's relief. I think even us children had had enough of a good thing.

Joyce Clifford,
Newent, Glos

Plant of the week

If you've alpine containers in your garden, then make sure you include a variety of Iris reticulata. The earliest of the irises to flower, these miniature beauties should be raised off the ground so you can enjoy them at eye level. They usually flower during late winter and early spring and produce blooms in a wide range of colours varying between the palest sky-blue to the deepest violet, each with a central yellow splash. They enjoy full sun but will cope with most soils as long as they're well-drained. H15cm (6in) AGM.

● **Tip** – propagate by dividing congested clumps of bulbs between mid-summer and early autumn.

Etiquette for Everybody
– 1920s' style –

On deportment…
'A stride of average length should be cultivated. A mincing shuffle as well as an ungainly stretch of the legs makes a pleasant air impossible.'

And another thing...

Tea is the leaf from the plant, camellia sinensis, a flowering evergreen shrub that grows in many countries around the world.

Wartime memories

Although she was a WREN, Mrs Mary Guile of Newcastle-upon-Tyne never went to sea

My parents weren't happy when at 17 I joined the Women's Royal Navy, having never been away from home before. I reported to the Admiralty in London before being transferred to Gillingham in Kent. Then training to be a WREN started. I enjoyed the marching and we also had discussions and seminars.

Later I was moved to South Kensington. The nearest I got to a ship was going down the Thames to Greenwich on the admiral's barge.

The bombing was dreadful in London, especially the doodlebugs, which were planes with small bombs that made a dreadful noise. The noise would suddenly stop, and you always looked up as they would glide or sometimes come straight down. If they were above you and coming straight down, you ran for your life to the nearest shelter. At night the underground station was full of people sleeping on the ground.

You saw lovely buildings one minute that were flattened the next. One night, all our windows were blown out and my friend was blown right out of one of them but, luckily, we weren't hurt much.

You often received letters from home saying that someone you knew had been killed. I met a sailor boy who was one of our neighbours and, as I was going on leave, he asked me to tell his mother that he was all right. I did, but a month later I heard that he had been killed at sea –

only 18 years old.

We had to have coupons to get clothes, and nylons were difficult to get unless you knew an American. We had to get a chitty signed, '1 pair stockings'. We would change the '1' to '2' but I got caught and was given 14 days scrubbing stairs, not allowed out. I didn't do that again!

♻ Keen to be green

Everyday ways to save the plane

- It's a waste to put all those carefully chosen Christmas cards in the dustbin. Check out your nearest Boots or W H Smith to see if they have a collection box for them. Some local council offices and Post Offices also provide this service.

- If you can't bear to part with the prettiest cards, cut them up to use as gift tags. Pretty bows and ribbons from parcels can be stored away and re-used. Carefully smooth and fold wrapping paper ready for next year's festive season.

- Don't just dump your wilting Christmas tree at the bottom of the garden, phone your local council to see if it has a scheme for collecting them to be shredded for compost.

- Instead of washing up after every meal, stack dirty crocks tidily and wash them all just once a day.

- There is no need to use more than one ring when cooking vegetables. Quickly cooked vegetables, such as cabbage or leeks, can be steamed above slower ones such as potatoes or carrots.

- Don't dismiss old-fashioned ideas – a knitted 'snake' draught excluder placed across the bottom of the door is still a very effective way to cut down on heating bills.

- Make a New Year's resolution to banish aerosol sprays from your home; they emit CFCs that damage the ozone layer and some experts believe they may also be harmful to asthma sufferers.

In the garden

- After the New Year celebrations are over, beer barrels can be sawn in half to make attractive tubs for plants.

Quiz

Test your knowledge with this fun quiz. If you get stuck the answers are at the bottom of the page.

PIC: REX FEATURES

1 How many sides does a pentagon have?

2 In what American state was Elvis Presley born?

3 What star sign begins on January 21?

4 Which author wrote The Thirty-Nine Steps?

5 Which actress played Alf Garnett's wife Elsie in Till Death Us Do Part?

6 Which famous Australian landmark do the Aborigines know as Uluru?

7 In which industry would a clapperboard be used?

8 Which famous American cartoonist created the Peanuts strip?

9 When in Rome, do what?

10 Which county is Canvey Island a part of?

11 How many furlongs are there in a mile?

12 Which famous square in London is home to Nelson's Column?

1 Five
2 Mississippi
3 Aquarius
4 John Buchan
5 Dandy Nichols
6 Ayer's Rock
7 The film industry
8 Charles Schulz
9 Do as the Romans do
10 Essex
11 Eight
12 Trafalgar Square

Decision Day by Eddi Woodbridge

Harold had no sense of time so it was left to Maud
to seize the moment before it passed forever

Maud stopped and riffled again through her shiny new crocodile handbag, a 25th birthday present from Mother and Father, to check she had the tickets safely tucked into the inside pocket. Taking them out, she reread the words for the umpteenth time, 'Choral Concert Wednesday 29th February 1928 – 7.30pm – Exeter Cathedral – price 2/6d'.

"Next Wednesday," she murmured to herself. "Wednesday! Shall I? Dare I? What will Mother say?" It had seemed an awfully good idea last night as she was dreamily brushing her hair before bed but now she was having second thoughts. She'd read of such things, but didn't personally know anyone who'd actually dared to do it. She didn't want to appear forward, or unladylike, but it was now or never. Wasn't it?

Biting her lip, she stood and thought a little longer. Then, coming to a decision, she took a deep breath and continued along the street towards the museum. Checking her reflection in Westaway's shop window as she walked by, Maud was mortified to see that the lining showed beneath the hem of her fur coat. Turning quickly, she headed towards Deller's café and made for the ladies' cloakroom, where she managed to hitch it up and pin it with three safety-pins from her handbag.

She ran her tortoiseshell comb through hair, dabbed some powder on her nose and applied another coat of Yardley's Pink Blush to her lips. Pulling on her gloves, she smiled at herself in the mirror, checked that her stocking seams were straight, then set off again towards the museum.

Entering the museum she found Harold. He was poring intently over the display of ammonites and belemnites in glass cases just inside the main hall, but he looked up with a smile when Maud softly called his name. "Will you be much longer?" Maud whispered. "I thought we might go to Deller's for lunch?"

Harold looked confused for a second, then exclaimed: "My goodness, is it that time already?" Maud smiled tolerantly. How long had she known him? It must be – what? – more than four years but, despite sporting an elegant gold watch on his wrist, he had absolutely no idea of time. Unless he was talking about geological eras, of course. In fact, sometimes Maud thought they were more real to him than the here and now. 'He probably doesn't even know what year this is, let alone the month,' Maud sighed to herself.

She was uncharacteristically quiet as they ate their oxtail soup followed by mutton stew, then steamed suet pudding with custard. Harold ate heartily as he told her how his first week in his new post of librarian had gone. "I feel I've really found my niche," he explained, "I'm sure I will still be enjoying it just as much on the day I retire."

Maud had to laugh. "That will be in…" she calculated, "in… 1975. I wonder what I will be doing then?"

"You, Miss Colson, will still be opening the minds of young students to the delights of Shakespeare, Chaucer and Milton, no doubt," Harold replied, "and looking as beautiful as ever, of course," he

*She didn't want to appear forward,
or unladylike, but it was now or never*

PIC: REX FEATURES

for the National Anthem at the end of the performance. They left by the west door of the cathedral and walked round through the close towards Southernhay.

The wind was from the north and Maud shivered as she snuggled into her fur coat. "Are you all right, my dear?" Harold enquired, giving her an anxious look.

"I'm - I'm…" Maud stopped suddenly in her tracks and turned to confront Harold's kind face. It was now or never. Had she the courage to do it?

Pushing a stray lock of hair back up under her cloche hat, and blushing furiously, she said in a rush: "Harold, I don't know if you're aware of it or not, but this year is a Leap Year. And today is the twenty-ninth of February, the day when it's customary for single young women to ask young men to marry them. So – Harold – will you marry me? Please?"

Forty-eight years later, a grey-haired couple looked up at the unchanging façade of the ancient cathedral and smiled at the memory of that unconventional proposal of marriage. Harold bent to kiss Maud tenderly then, strolling arm-in-arm towards Southernhay, they talked contentedly of their retirement plans – with all the time in the world to read, enjoy concerts and visit art galleries together. The world was still their oyster.

added with a shy smile. "We will continue to meet in the museum on Saturday mornings, as we have done today, dine at Deller's or The White Hart and discuss all manner of topics – music, literature, art – that are of great interest to us both. The world is our oyster."

Maud's smile wavered, and she looked down at her lap. Then, brightening, she made a momentous decision. Opening the bag, she said gaily: "I managed to get some tickets for Wednesday's concert. I do hope you can come?" She drew out the tickets and waved them

at Harold.

He looked delighted, so Maud added: "Mother said would you like to come to tea before the concert. Then we can go on from there." Mother hadn't actually said any such thing, but Maud knew it would be all right – both her parents were very fond of the quietly charming young man. "Mother has made some delicious winter fruits jelly," she added by way of an added incentive.

The concert was even better than they'd expected, and Maud felt transported to another world as they rose to their feet

February 2006

Wednesday

1

Yours February 01 issue on sale

Thursday

2

Friday

3

Saturday

4

Sunday

5

Monday

6

Tuesday

7

Wednesday

8

Thursday

9

Friday

10

Cheltenham Folk Festival

Saturday

11

Cheltenham Folk Festival

Sunday

12

Cheltenham Folk Festival

Monday

13

Tuesday

14

St Valentine's Day

Wednesday

15

Thursday

16

Friday

17

Saturday

18

Sunday

19

Monday

20

Tuesday

21

Wednesday

22

Thursday

23

Friday

24

Saturday

25

Sunday

26

Monday

27

Tuesday

28

Shrove Tuesday (Lent begins)

PIC: BRIAN HARRIS/REX FEATURES

Flavour of the month

Grey February days are brightened by gleaming white drifts of snowdrops in woodland and hedgerows. The flower's delicate appearance belies its toughness, thrusting its way above ground whatever the weather. Look in your local paper for private gardens near you that are open at weekends for snowdrop walks.

After an enjoyable expedition to admire the early heralds of spring, come home to a nice hot cup of tea, a slice of cake – and a browse through the travel brochures.

Whether your dreams are of blue Caribbean skies or a cottage hideaway in Devon, now is the time to cheer yourself up with the prospect of a delightful summer holiday to come.

This is a good time of the year for compulsive hoarders to clear out those cupboards and drawers that are stuffed with long-forgotten bits and pieces. Junk items can go straight into black bin bags and the rest sorted into carrier bags ready to be taken to the charity shop. And the same goes for your

wardrobe – any clothes that you haven't worn for two years won't be missed and you'll be glad of the extra hanging space.

Don't dismiss Valentine's Day on the 14th as being just for young sweethearts. Romantics of all ages know that a warm hug and a reminder 'you are still the love of my life' are worth more than any number of shop-bought red roses. (But, of course, a box of chocolates and a candlelit dinner for two will be warmly received as well!)

My Mum

This photograph is of my Mother, Joyce Gleeson and myself in 1945. My mother loved dogs (probably more than people) – she walked mine even after the age of 91. She was a very active lady and walked at least one-and-a-half miles every day, refusing to use a stick and living alone right until the very end. She knew a few days before she died at the age of 98 that I was waiting for a new puppy; I had a flat-coated retriever on order, having just lost one.

In the photograph I received a slight reprimand for calling Nicky, the Dalmatian (not a good one – wrong spots!) to 'kiss'. You can see the look of surprise on my mother's face.

Oonagh M Gleeson,
Needham Market, Suffolk

Oonagh receiving a 'doggy kiss'

Etiquette for Everybody
– 1920s' style –

On dinner parties…
'Do not scold the attendants if they are slow or have the misfortune to break something. The kitchen is the place for recriminations.'

TOP TIP

Next time you vacuum, add a cotton wool ball soaked with a few drops of aromatherapy oil, like geranium or lavender into your vacuum cleaner bag. A lovely smell!

✛YOUR GOOD HEALTH✛

Eye, eye
Do your eyes often feel dry and gritty? They produce fewer tears to keep them lubricated as we age, while cold winds and central heating can worsen the problem. Drink two litres of water daily and avoid dehydrating drinks like coffee and alcohol. Upping your intake of foods rich in essential fats, such as avocados, mackerel, salmon and nuts, can also help.

A treasured memento

One of my most treasured possessions is a stained and varnished wooden box, measuring $7^3/_4$ins long, $4^1/_4$ins wide and $2^1/_2$ins deep. It's perfectly crafted with mortice and tenon joints.

I enjoyed embroidery from a very early age and my father made me the box to hold my silks. Shortly after giving me my treasure, and two months before my 12th birthday, my father died in January 1951.

My late husband once commented on how much I treasured my little box and I told him the story attached to it. He was most impressed with the accuracy and workmanship it had taken to create my box but I think it is the love and thoughtfulness which went into the making, which makes it my most treasured memento.

Mrs Hilda Yates, Preston

Plant of the week

Galanthus nivalis, the common snowdrop, is a must-have plant in every garden because it heralds the end of winter. Completely hardy, it loves the dappled shade beneath trees and will cope in most soils, even heavy clay. When the clumps have become overcrowded, lift the plants immediately after flowering, divide and replant. H15cm (6in) AGM.
● **Tip** – Avoid buying bulbs. Instead order plants 'in the green' because these are quicker to establish.

My Prayer

I this is a prayer I have written. The teaching of Jesus in a capsule, maybe?

Thank you, Lord
Grant me a calm and peaceful day
A cheek to turn the other way
A quiet moment, just to say
Thank you, Lord
Mr Don Robinson, Bury, Lancs

And another thing...

'Never trust a man who, when he's alone in a room with a tea cosy, doesn't try it on.'

Billy Connolly

A RECIPE FOR YOU

Bramley and Apricot Crumble
(Serves 4)

For the apple
● 700 g (1½ lb) Bramley apples
● 2 tablespoons lemon juice
● 75 g (3 oz) sugar
● 25 g (1 oz) butter
● Grated rind of 1 lemon
● 450 g (approx 1 lb) can of apricot halves, in juice

For the crumble topping
● 200 g (7 oz) plain white flour
● 100 g (approx 4 oz) butter or margarine
● 50 g (2 oz) sugar
● 25 g (1 oz) rolled oats

1 Preheat oven to 190°C, 375°F, Gas Mark 5, 10 minutes before baking.
2 Peel the Bramley apples, core and slice thickly. Place in a saucepan with the lemon juice and sugar.
3 Cook covered for 8 minutes or until just tender, add the butter and stir until melted. Remove from the heat.
4 Cut the apricots in half, add to the apples and the lemon rind with 2 tablespoons of the juice from the apricots, then place in an ovenproof dish.
5 Sift the flour into a mixing bowl and rub in the butter or margarine until the mixture resembles fine breadcrumbs. Stir in the sugar and rolled oats.
6 Spoon onto the top of the apple mixture and pat down gently. Bake in the preheated oven for 25-30 minutes or until the crumble topping is golden. Serve warm with cream, custard or ice cream. RECIPE COURTESY BRAMLEY APPLE INFORMATION SERVICE

A treasured memento

Wrapped in tissue in a box of treasured mementoes is a small, yellow Dinky toy – a Volvo dump truck.

In the 1970s my husband drove a Volvo on motorway construction sites. We travelled all over the country, living in a tiny 12ft caravan. Parking in a farmer's field or on the side of a half-built road, we stayed for a few months or a few days, moving at a moment's notice.

Life wasn't easy, especially with the arrival of our daughter. A five-gallon water container was all we had to last a day, so washing nappies was a problem. Some mornings we had ice on top of the blankets on the bed, and the door of the caravan had to be forced open because of frost.

In the summer it was too hot inside and too dusty outside but we all survived, and the other drivers loved having a small baby on site to spoil.

Unfortunately, my marriage ended when we finally settled in a house, the gypsy in my husband calling him back to his caravan. I remarried several years later to a wonderful man who took my daughter as his own and we are sharing our years happily together.

But whenever I unwrap that little toy I can smell again the dust, diesel and the open road…
Mrs Gwen Spain, Plymouth

Plant of the week

Many hellebores start producing their gently nodding flowers in January and carry on until late April – and there are masses of colourful hybrids to choose between. The majority produce large saucer-shaped flowers and one hybrid which is slightly more unusual, and the result of extensive cross-breeding, is H ballardiae which has short stems of white blooms tinted brownish-pink in bud above silver-veined leaves. H30cm (1ft).
● **Tip** – Avoid moving plants once they've settled in, as they take a while to re-establish

And another thing...

"That's the fastest time ever run – but it's not as fast as the world record."   *David Coleman*

Etiquette for Everybody
– 1920s' style –

On sitting in company…
'When you sit down, sit down comfortably, but not lackadaisically. And do not appear ill at ease. And do not tilt the chair or sprawl your arms over a settee; and men should not remove their bowler hats.'

A RECIPE FOR YOU

Teviotdale Pie

- 1 tablespoon oil
- 450 g (approx 1 lb) lean minced beef or lamb
- 1 medium onion, chopped
- 2 tablespoons dark muscovado sugar
- 300 ml (10 fl oz) beef stock
- 2 teaspoons Worcestershire sauce
- Salt and pepper
- 225 g (8 oz) self-raising flour
- 25 g (1 oz) cornflour
- 75 g (3 oz) shredded suet
- 300 ml (10 fl oz) milk

1 Heat the oil in a pan and cook the minced meat for a few minutes until beginning to brown.
2 Add the onion and continue to cook for another 5 minutes until soft. Stir in the sugar, stock and Worcestershire sauce.
3 Season to taste, and simmer for 20 minutes.
4 Preheat the oven to 180°C, 350°F, or Gas Mark 4.
5 Spoon into a 1.1 litre pie dish.
6 Put the flour, cornflour and suet in a mixing bowl and gradually beat in the milk to form a thick batter. Season well with salt and pepper.
7 Spoon the batter over the meat mixture and cook for 30-35 minutes until risen and golden.

RECIPE COURTESY BILLINGTON'S

Whoosh, there goes another one!

It had been snowing for more than two days, the garden was under a cold, thick white blanket. Nobody wanted to venture very far outside, but the birds' container on our apple tree

Nancy preparing another snowball

needed topping up. So, wellies on, woolly hat, scarf, jacket and mitts, out I gingerly stepped.

Suddenly, an unbidden urge made me desperately need to throw snowballs everywhere, and shout, 'Whooosh' with excited glee as they went flying about all over the garden. Now, considering this last abandonment was when our children were small, and now me being an OAP, this was quite inexplicable behaviour!

The photograph was secretly snapped by my husband…

Nancy Lowther,
Cliftonville, Kent

✚YOUR GOOD HEALTH✚

Clear away colds

When you get a respiratory infection such as a cold or flu, the body sends virus-fighting white blood cells to the site. But these also attack the mucous membranes of the nose, throat and lungs, leading to irritation and excess mucous – and resulting in a runny nose and cough. The herb pelargonium, from health food stores, can prevent viruses and bacteria clinging to mucus membranes, so take 100ug three times daily at the first sign of symptoms, and continue taking for 48 hours after the infection has cleared.

February 13-19

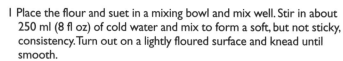

A RECIPE FOR YOU

Sussex Pond Pudding
(Serves 6-8)

- 300 g (approx 10 oz) self-raising flour
- 150 g (5 oz) vegetable suet
- 150 g (5 oz) dark brown soft sugar
- 100 g (4 oz) butter
- 2 whole lemons, preferably unwaxed
- Custard to serve

1 Place the flour and suet in a mixing bowl and mix well. Stir in about 250 ml (8 fl oz) of cold water and mix to form a soft, but not sticky, consistency. Turn out on a lightly floured surface and knead until smooth.

2 Reserve one-third of the pastry and roll the remaining pastry out on a lightly floured surface and use to line a lightly oiled 1.2 litre (2 pint) pudding basin. Ensure that the pastry fits snugly in the basin and trim edges neatly.

3 Place half the dark brown soft sugar and half the butter, cut into cubes in the pudding basin. Lightly scrub the lemons and prick all over with a skewer. Place on top of the dark brown soft sugar and butter. Sprinkle with the remaining sugar, then the rest of the butter cut into cubes.

4 Roll the reserved pastry out to a circle for the lid, dampen edges and place lid in the position. Seal edges firmly, then cover with a double sheet of greaseproof paper, then either a pudding cloth or tin foil. (Put a pleat in the centre of the greaseproof paper or tin foil to allow for expansion.)

5 Place in the top of a steamer over a pan of gently simmering water and steam for 4 hours. Top up with water as necessary. Serve straight from the basin with custard.

RECIPE COURTESY TATE & LYLE

TOP TIP

Slice unwaxed lemons thinly and cut into quarters, put in ice trays with a little water. Ice and lemon supplied in one go.

And another thing...

'Life is rather like a tin of sardines. We're all of us looking for the key.'
Alan Bennett

My Prayer

Maureen's affirmation
Every day in every way, I am getting better and better
I relax in mind and body that the spirit may operate
And make of me a balanced being.
I have a healthy mind in a healthy body and I enjoy life.
Wonderful things now come to me in wonderful ways
And I am truly thankful
Maureen Harrison, Broughton Astley, Leics

✚YOUR GOOD HEALTH✚

Fight off flakes

A dry, itchy scalp can be irritating – and embarrassing. But you can beat it with a homemade astringent scalp tonic, according to trichologist Philip Kingsley. He advises shaking together a mouthwash of your choice with an equal quantity of witch hazel. Shampoo and towel dry your hair, then sprinkle the tonic over your scalp, rub it in, and style your hair as normal.

A treasured memento

Most precious to me are the words from a Valentine card, written and sent to me by my then boyfriend, Arthur.

He wrote it on a lovely card in 1954. We married in 1957, so the Valentine is 51 years old! I can still say the words off by heart, and we are still very much in love, now aged 70 and 72. I have the Valentine in front of me as I write.

Sweet as the breeze through the whispering trees,
Bright as the stars in the night,
Memories of you so constant and true,
Shine with a radiance bright.
Take them I pray this Valentine's Day,
Dearest, this word from my heart,
Good fortune uphold you till my arms enfold you,
Forever, and never to part.

Mrs Jackie B Sheppard, Bristol

Plant of the week

Eranthis hyemalis, the winter aconite, has bright yellow flowers backed by a pretty ruff of green leaflets. It flowers in late winter and early spring and quickly produces a carpet of colour, especially if planted in light shade with plenty of leaf mould. It's an ideal companion for snowdrops and cyclamen. H8cm (3in).

● Tip - Water the plants regularly during their first season.

My Mum

My mother, Gladys, was 103 when she died and was the oldest person in the town. She had a remarkable memory and could remember back to 1903 when she was two years old. My abiding memory of her was her pride in remembering in detail her childhood, teenage years and working days. She was well known in the town for her reminiscences, and was thrilled when asked to speak at various groups. She was highly delighted when a sketch was written and performed extensively in the area, based on her experiences. She really was a wonderful woman.

Gladys on her 100th birthday, with a bunch of roses and her message from the Queen

Mrs Bernice Freestone, Market Harborough

A treasured memento

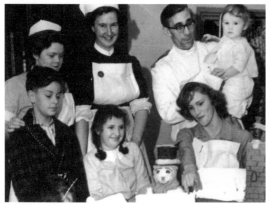

Angela (pointing to the snow scene) in the children's surgical ward, 1959

A long ribbon of paper – my first wage slip for the glorious amount of £12 15s 10d – is my treasure. I thought it was a fortune! My wages for my first month's work at the local hospital as a cadet nurse, working in the general office.

My first day hadn't got off to a good start, as I had to visit the casualty department as a patient. Running an errand for my Nana before going to work, I'd badly grazed my right arm and removed my thumbnail when I fell off my bike.

So in casualty I had to suffer the indignity of a tetanus injection in the bottom, and have my arm bandaged from thumb-tip to elbow. This caused a great deal of mirth among the staff who said I certainly knew how to make an entrance.

Despite this, I managed to work during my first month and received a small, brown envelope containing my wages. Even after giving my Nan my board and lodge money, there was still plenty to buy a lipstick I'd wanted, which was a shade worn by model Jean Shrimpton.

Mrs Angela J Wilson, South Ruislip

TOP TIP

Your TV and video can use as much electricity on standby as they do switched on, so unplug them at night.

A RECIPE FOR YOU

Thai Beef Mussaman
(Serves 3-4)
- 450 g (approx 1lb) lean beef braising steak, cut into cubes
- 15 ml (1 tablespoon) oil
- 1 onion, sliced
- 1 red chilli, deseeded and sliced
- 30 ml (2 tablespoons) red Thai curry paste
- 1 tablespoon brown sugar
- 1 tablespoon tamarind paste
- 2 medium potatoes, peeled and cut into large chunks
- 400 ml can (approx) coconut milk
- 250 ml (nearly ½ pt) pineapple juice
- 1 small aubergine, cut into wedges
- 30 ml (2 tablespoons) peanut butter
- Fresh coriander

1 Heat the oven to 180°C, 350°F, Gas Mark 4. Heat the oil in a large saucepan. Add the lean beef braising steak, the sliced onion and the chilli, and cook until meat has browned. Then add the red Thai curry paste, brown sugar, tamarind paste, potato chunks, coconut milk and the pineapple juice.

2 Cover and cook in a preheated oven for 1½ hours. Remove from oven and add the peanut butter and the aubergine wedges. Cover and return to the oven and cook for 30 minutes or until meat is tender. Sprinkle with coriander and sliced chillies.

3 Serve with sticky coconut rice (cook basmati rice in water and coconut milk).

- This recipe contains nuts

RECIPE COURTESY BRITISH MEAT INFORMATION SERVICE

All bets were on!

An early recollection was my mother discussing 'the old king (George VI) dying' and I vaguely remember seeing the newsreel pictures of the young Princess Elizabeth returning home as Queen.

I remember, too, watching history in the making on a tiny nine-inch television screen and thinking that the beaming Queen of Tonga looked great fun.

I can't ever recall being bored, with marbles, hopscotch and conkers in the autumn; cricket, skipping, spinning tops in the summer, and we made rag mats and raffia baskets.

We weren't angels, though! A favourite game of mine – called Thunder and Lightning – was to knock like thunder on people's doors, then ran like lightning as soon as anyone answered!

My brothers used to like a flutter on the horses each Saturday and would send me with their bets. It wasn't until years later I realised I was breaking the law. However, the wages of sin were very good – my brothers always made sure I had a sixpenny bet as well – and the horses usually won!

Christine James, Rugeley, Staffs

Plant of the week

Corylopsis pauciflora, the winter hazel, is a great choice for a shady position. Its popularity owes much to the bright primrose-yellow flowers which have a cowslip-like scent that it produces early in the year. It needs acidic, well-drained conditions so if your soil is alkaline, plant it in a large container using ericaceous compost. H 1.8m (6ft). AGM.

● **Tip** – Choose a lightly shaded part of the garden so the blooms are protected from spring frosts.

✚ YOUR GOOD HEALTH ✚

Breathe easy

Correct breathing can make a real difference to your wellbeing. Most of us only breathe with the top section of our lungs, which can lead to feelings of stress and tiredness. Instead, try sitting in a comfortable position and inhaling deeply through your nose into your abdomen so that it inflates. Then breathe out slowly through your nostrils. Practise this deep abdominal breathing for ten minutes each day, and use it to calm you down next time you get wound up!

Etiquette for Everybody
– 1920s' style –

On correct dress...
'Ladies should not remove their gloves when making an afternoon call; such an act would suggest a long stay.'

And another thing...

Did you know that 'Rhythm' is one of the longest English words without vowels?

Wartime memories

Mrs Andrina Cossey of Falmouth spent the war years in India

My parents were working in India at the outbreak of the war and spent the duration there. They gave soldiers' tea parties in their lovely Delhi garden. The men, mostly on their way to Burma, welcomed the break after a long sea voyage in cramped troop ships. They tucked into the lavish spread; cream cakes, buns and sandwiches laid out on white-draped tables under the neem trees.

I was five and my sister was three; two little fair-haired girls in their Sunday best, starched white dresses with poppies and matching scarlet shoes. Our straight hair was tied in curling rags the night before a party. I was a tomboy who hated all that and was much happier in shorts but we had to dress up for such occasions.

Later, American soldiers came to tea and we were introduced to chewing gum and waffles. I loved the warm, crisp pancakey taste with the holes dripping with golden syrup.

My father was deputy director of food and supplies and my mother collected money for the Red Cross. We were not left out of the war effort. We wore little nurses' uniforms – white caps and aprons with red crosses – and our 'patient' was a small boy covered from head to toe in bandages. The three of us went round in a tonga, a horse-drawn carriage, rattling our collecting boxes.

In May 1945 we travelled home on a troopship crowded with returning families; there were 12 women and 12 children

Andrina with her young sister, dressed in their Sunday best

to a large cabin. It was a great contrast to our rather sheltered life and I revelled in the deck games and the company of other children, although it was much more of a strain for my mother with the lack of privacy. The war with Japan was not yet over so we had boat drill and anti-aircraft practice but eventually reached home safely.

Keen to be green
Everyday ways to save the planet

- It's not always essential to use harsh chemical cleaners for tough cleaning jobs – distilled vinegar will remove lime stains from ceramic tiles or around the base of taps.

- Old bedlinen converts to handy dustsheets to protect the furniture when you are decorating, or cut up sheets and pillow cases to make cleaning cloths or dusters.

- Bicycles can, quite literally, be recycled! The charity Re-Cycle sends them to developing countries where they can be repaired and enjoy a second lease of life. Website: www.re-cycle.org.

- Books in good condition are always welcomed by charity shops and secondhand book dealers. If books are too battered to be read, see if your council has a book bank to supply recycled paper manufacturers.

- Save electricity by turning your TV off every night instead of leaving it on standby (check that the red light doesn't show).

- Car batteries can be recycled; take them to a scrap metal merchant, garage or your local authority recycling centre.

- Don't leave the cold water tap running while you are cleaning your teeth. Another useful tip – by immersing the tube in warm water, you will be able to extract the last squeeze of toothpaste more easily.

In the garden
- Use old wool or cotton carpets upside-down as a mulch and to suppress weeds. Carpets made from man-made fibres and underlay are hardwearing and can be cut into strips for use as paths in parts of the garden that are not on show. They also make effective weed suppressants.

What's in a name?

Gilly Pickup takes a
lighthearted look at some
unusual place names...

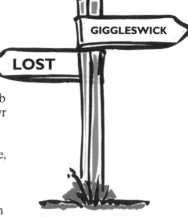

How would you feel about living in Pity Me or Lost? Pity Me is a village in County Durham said to be the site of a small lake or 'mere' and that the name means Petit Mere.

The tiny hamlet of Lost is in Scotland's Cairngorm Mountains; the name comes from a Celtic word meaning 'inn'. Today the hamlet has only a few houses, a war memorial and a farm. Because of its unusual name, Lost has suffered serious problems since it was mentioned in guidebooks several years ago because jokers kept stealing Lost's signposts. Not surprisingly, the locals were thoroughly fed up with having to fork out around £100 for each replacement, so they've now changed the name to Lost Farm, in an effort to solve the problem.

It must be confusing if you live in America – the one in Cambridgeshire, England that is. Or if you hail from Ireland which is actually in Bedfordshire, or worse still if you say you're a Californian, because apart from the one in the USA, its namesake can be found in Buckinghamshire, and also near Falkirk. And, if that wasn't enough, there's New York in Lincolnshire, and Jericho in Angus.

Llanhyfryddawelllehynafolyb arcudprindanfygythiadtrienusyr hafnauole is the new name given to the village of Llanfynydd in Carmarthenshire, Wales. Local residents are worried about the effects on wildlife of a proposed wind farm, so renamed the village on July 19, 2004.

In English, the name means, 'a quiet beautiful village, an historic place with rare kite under threat from wretched blades'. Locals are afraid it will threaten three endangered species of bird – red kite, curlew and skylark. The name was also chosen as it is longer than the current longest name in Britain which is Llanfairpwllgwyngyll-gogerychwyrndrobwllllantysilio gogogoch in Anglesey and would thus generate publicity for their cause.

Meanwhile, the shortest place name is probably Ae, a small village in Scotland's Dumfries and Galloway, lying within the forest of the same name.

Giggleswick near Settle in North Yorkshire (meaning 'dwelling or (dairy) farm of a man called Gukel or Gichel') suggests a place with a large smile on its face, just as Little Snoring in Norfolk sounds peaceful. And The Land of Nod near Grayshott, Hampshire must be a chill-out destination?

Whether or not the Hertfordshire village of Nasty is true to its name goes unrecorded but on balance it might be better to live in Ugley, a village in Essex, as it's pronounced something nearer to 'usley'.

You'd get a great deal of sympathy if someone asked where your home town was and you shrugged, No Place. But in fact No Place is indeed a place, a hamlet near the town of Stanley in County Durham. The origins of the name are uncertain but whispers are that it was so named to try to confuse the tax man. Some years ago, when the local council wanted to change the name to Co-operative Villas, the locals protested. They were horrified at the thought of all the signs pointing to No Place being removed. After all, there is No Place like home, is there?

As William Shakespeare said, 'What's in a name?' I suppose the answer to that depends on the name!

March 2006

Wednesday

1 **Yours** March 1 issue on sale, St David's Day

Thursday

2

Friday

3

Saturday

4

Sunday

5

Monday

6

Tuesday

7

Wednesday

8

Thursday

9 Crufts Dog Show, NEC, Birmingham

Friday

10 Crufts Dog Show, NEC, Birmingham

Saturday

11 Crufts Dog Show, NEC, Birmingham

Sunday

12 Crufts Dog Show, NEC, Birmingham

Monday

13

Tuesday

14

Wednesday

15

Thursday

16

Friday

17 St Patrick's Day (Bank Holiday in N Ireland)

Saturday

18

Sunday

19

Monday

20

Tuesday

21

Wednesday

22

Thursday

23

Friday

24

Saturday

25

Sunday

26   Mothering Sunday
British Summer Time begins, clocks go forward

Monday

27

Tuesday

28

Wednesday

29   **Yours** March 29 issue on sale

Thursday

30

Friday

31

Flavour of the month

If the wind howls around the house eaves this month, cheer up! Tradition has it that a windy March foretells a fine May. So batten down the hatches and make plans for warmer months to come.

It won't be too long before we are slipping into lighter summer clothing, so now is the time to indulge in some beauty treatments in readiness for sleeveless dresses and sandals. Bring a glow to your skin by making an exfoliating body scrub part of your bathtime routine. And pamper your feet with a regular pedicure. When using hand cream, don't forget to rub some on your feet, as well. Tone up those muscles with a daily walk – just 15 minutes will make a real difference.

Nothing tastes better than vegetables freshly picked from your own garden and by the end of the month you should be able to make a start on this year's crop by planting beans and peas straight in the ground. Parsnips, leeks and carrots can also be started now.

Although Simnel cake with its topping of 12 marzipan balls for each of the apostles has become an Easter treat, it was traditionally associated with Mother's Day. As Simnel Sunday and Mother's Day both fall on 26th March this year, what better excuse to bake a celebration cake for a deserving Mum.

Along with the cake, present her with a glorious bunch of daffodils. Sported by Welsh folk on the first of March (St David's Day), their golden trumpets add an air of irrepressible gaiety to the month.

PIC: PER LINDGREN/REX FEATURES

My Mum

Jennie's mum, Jane Ann

My most vivid memory of my Mother is of a black, winter morning at 5am. The windows rattled, buffeted by a fierce wind and slashed by driving rain, as I lay in bed warm and guilty. Downstairs, Mum was leaving the cold terraced house to go to work. There were no buses for early morning shift workers so Mum faced a lonely two-mile walk battling the elements in the dark, through the field to the hospital where she worked as a kitchen assistant.

And she did it for me. It was 1956 and I was 16 and at High School. My parents were determined to give me the opportunity to fulfil an ambition to become a teacher. The memory encapsulates Mum's love and commitment to her family of three girls.

Mrs Jennie Barker, Pontefract

A treasured memento

The little treasure that I couldn't part with is an inch-high crucifix and chain. My husband gave it to me about 30 years ago and it has had several adventures, including this one:

Cecilia wearing her cross and chain

We went by train to Shepperton for a wedding, and had to change at Clapham Junction where we sat on a bench until the train arrived. While travelling I realised I'd lost the cross and chain. Coming home after the reception eight hours later, again on Clapham Junction, we looked all around and there it was under the seat where we'd sat!

Mrs Cecilia Ralph, Crawley

Plant of the week

Hyacinths are the best air freshener you can buy and so much better than artificial shop-bought ones because they're completely natural. Although prepared (temperature-treated to encourage early flowering) bulbs flower at Christmas if planted during September, hyacinths normally flower in early spring and are available in garden centres now.

● **Tip** – Old prepared hyacinths which bloomed at Christmas can be planted out in the garden where they will flower again the following spring.

Apricot Torte (Wheatfree)

- 3 medium eggs
- 100 g (4 oz) golden caster sugar
- 50 g (2 oz) ground almonds
- 25 g (1 oz) cornflour, sifted
- 2-3 drops of almond essence

For the Filling:

- 2 x 396 g cans apricot halves in juice, drained
- 15 ml (1 tablespoon) brandy
- 1 x 11 g (approx 1/2 oz) sachet of powdered gelatine
- 50 g (2 oz) Golden Caster sugar
- 2 medium egg whites
- 300 ml (approx 1/2 pint) double cream

1 Preheat oven to 190°C, 375°F, Gas Mark 5. Grease a 23 cm (9 ins) spring-clip tin; line it with baking parchment.
2 To make the sponge, place eggs and sugar in a large bowl over a pan of hot water. Whisk the mixture until thick enough to leave a ribbon trail. Fold in ground almonds, cornflour and almond essence with 30 ml (2 tablespoons) hot water. Pour into prepared tin and bake for 20-25 minutes or until sponge springs back when lightly touched.
3 When the sponge is cool, remove from cake tin. Line a 20 cm (8 inch) spring-clip tin with clear film. Then, with the tin base as a guide, trim the sponge to fit the tin. Cut sponge in half horizontally and place one half in the base of lined tin. Arrange enough apricots over sponge base to cover, sprinkle over brandy and set aside.
4 For the filling, sprinkle gelatine over 45 ml (3 tablespoons) cold water in a small bowl and leave until spongy, then stand the bowl in a pan of hot water and stir until dissolved. Leave to cool. Place remaining apricots in food processor with caster sugar, then blend until smooth. Transfer to a bowl.
5 Whisk egg whites and cream in separate bowl until just stiff. Working quickly, stir the cold gelatine into the puréed apricots, then fold in the cream and egg whites.
6 Pour mixture over the apricot halves. Chill for 1 hour. Place second sponge on top and chill for a further 2 hours. Serve in wedges dusted with icing sugar.

- This recipe contains nuts

RECIPE COURTESY BILLINGTON'S

And another thing...

'Opinions are like armpits: Everybody has two of them and they stink most of the time.'

Anonymous

+YOUR GOOD HEALTH+

A pain in the head?

Try not to reach for the painkillers every time you get a headache. Instead, lie in a darkened room with a hot towel across your forehead, and try massaging the webbed area between your thumb and index finger – this is an acupressure point believed in Chinese medicine to help relieve headaches.

Etiquette for Everybody
– 1920s' style –

On gentleman callers...

'The hostess, in offering to take a caller's hat and stick, is clearly suggesting that she wishes his stay to be protracted. If he then outlasts his welcome, she can only blame herself'.

TOP TIP

To clean up shards of broken glass safely, put on some rubber gloves and use some masking tape to pick up the glass pieces.

My Mum

Marlene today

Marlene and her family watching the new television

This black and white photograph was taken about 50 years ago, my mum in the background and me cuddling my brother, with one of my elder sisters. This was a special day because we'd rented a television and you can see the amazement in our faces.

My lovely mum looked after us on very little money but we always had proper meals and warm, clean beds. Quite often Mum could only make up the beds at night, as she only had the coal fire to dry them with. I loved laying in bed and Mum shaking out the fresh sheet over, making up the bed, and tucking me in.

My mum was a real treasure and I carry her love with me every day.

Mrs Marlene Brown, Sittingbourne, Kent

And another thing...

'Now I'm over 50 my doctor says I should get more exercise. I said, All right, I'll drive with the car window open.'   *Angus Walker*

Plant of the week

Festuca glauca is one of the most popular grasses among gardeners because its steely blue leaves look lovely all year round. It's great for providing structural interest in borders – albeit on a small scale – or on a rockery and also looks attractive in containers. Plants develop their most intense coloration when kept dry in summer. Plant in a sunny position in moist but well-drained soil. H30cm (1ft).

● **Tip** – Divide plants in spring, removing all brown leaves from around the base, then replant immediately.

Etiquette for Everybody
– 1920s' style –

On conversation…
'…Should the conversation flag, do not get interested in the pictures and ornaments around the room, as you would those in a museum.'

A RECIPE FOR YOU

Spiced Chick Peas

- 4 tablespoons oil
- 2 onions, finely chopped
- 2 cloves garlic, finely chopped
- 2 teaspoons ground cumin
- 2 teaspoons ground coriander
- 1 teaspoon ground turmeric
- 2 teaspoons ground paprika
- Pinch cayenne pepper
- ½ teaspoon salt
- 2 x 400 g (14 oz) tins chickpeas, drained
- 2 tablespoons tomato purée
- 2 tablespoons molasses sugar
- 150 ml (¼ pint) water or vegetable stock
- Salt and pepper to taste

1 Heat the oil in a pan over a low heat.
2 Add the onions, garlic, spices and salt and cook until the onions are soft but not browned.
3 Stir in the chickpeas, tomato purée and molasses sugar, then pour in the water or stock and bring to the boil.
4 Cover and simmer for 30 minutes.
5 Season to taste. Turn into a large serving bowl or individual bowls and serve with warm crusty bread, rice or a green salad. Serves 2-3.

RECIPE COURTESY BILLINGTON'S

Sorry, George can't come...

In 1947 I was working as Matron's maid at a hospital in Farnham, Surrey. One evening after work, I had a date with a Welsh soldier called George.

When I got to our meeting place, his colleague Harold had turned up to say George couldn't meet me because he was on duty.

We decided to go for a drink and during the course of the evening Harold said he didn't think George was being fair to me because he wasn't on duty but out with another girl.

I never saw George again, but that evening started a lifetime with Harold, we were married the following year and last year we celebrated out 58th wedding anniversary. Thank you, George!

Mrs N Heard, Guildford

✚YOUR GOOD HEALTH✚

Shape Up
Want to lose a few pounds in time for spring? Forget faddy diets, the best approach is to eat little and often, say nutritionists. Cup your hands with your fingers together – each meal should fit into that area. Between meals, eat small snacks combining protein with carbohydrate, such as oatcakes with hummus, or an apple with a few nuts – this will stop you getting ravenous and reaching for huge plates of food come lunch or dinner.

TOP TIP

Use melted ice from the fridge tray as sterilised water for your steam iron.

A RECIPE FOR YOU

Sugar Cube Pecan Muffins
(Makes 12)

- 300 g (approx 11 oz) plain flour
- 2 teaspoons baking powder
- 150 g (5 oz) light brown soft cane sugar
- 75g (3 oz) pecans, roughly chopped
- ½ teaspoon mixed spice
- 1 egg
- 1 teaspoon vanilla extract
- 225 ml (between ¼ and ½ pint) milk
- 50 g (2 oz) butter, melted
- 4 tablespoons strong black coffee
- 12 sugar cubes

1 Preheat the oven to 200°C, 400°F, Gas Mark 6. Sift the flour and baking powder into a large bowl and stir in the brown sugar, pecans and spice.
2 Crack the egg into a separate bowl and whisk in the vanilla, milk and melted butter.
3 Stir the liquid into the dry ingredients, taking care not to over mix. Spoon the mixture into a 12-hole greased or paper-cased muffin tin.
4 Dip the sugar cubes into the coffee, then push into the centre of each muffin. Bake for 15-20 minutes until well-risen and just firm.
- **TIP**: The sugar cubes begin to dissolve as soon as they're dipped in the coffee, so push them into the muffin at once. RECIPE COURTESY TATE & LYLE

My Prayer

This verse was given to me by an old friend before she died.
An Old World Creed
I believe in all things beautiful –
the beauty of simple things
I believe in music where the melody is quickly found
And in poems that sound like song

I believe in books that hold no ugly thought
In pictures that rest the eye and soothe the senses
And in plays that keep the heart young

Little things delight me:
A sunbeam on a blade of grass
A dewdrop in the heart of a flower
A daisy with a rosy frill

I believe in joy and quick laughter
In sentiment, in love
I believe in all things beautiful
I believe in God

Mrs Catherine Wylde, Sale

And another thing...

Louth in Lincolnshire is the most northerly town in the world sited on the Greenwich, or Prime, meridian. It also has the highest church steeple in England.

Etiquette for Everybody
– 1920s' style –

On outstaying your welcome...
'When it is time to go, go. The visitor who leaves too soon or who will not take his departure is a nuisance.'

+YOUR GOOD HEALTH+

Kick start your spring cleaning

Piles of paper and mounds of old clothes drain your vitality, according to feng shui, so get tough and dump everything you don't either need or love.

- Be strict about clothes – send anything you haven't worn in the last year to a charity shop.
- Start small – begin by sorting out your handbag or underwear drawer, and go through each room bit by bit.

Sleepy Stella!

Stella enjoying creature comforts

This is our rescue dog, Stella. With a lot of hard work and a never-ending supply of love and cuddles to help her forget her bad start in life, she has now become 'our little girl in a fur coat'.

Stella likes to sit on the bench in the park and loves the comfort of a bed. If she can get upstairs at any time, she makes straight for my son's bed and, as you can see, likes to get under the covers.

Betty Brereton, Cheshire

Plant of the week

Anemone blanda has delightful daisy-like flowers, and comes in a wide range of colours including blue, purple, maroon, pink and white. It enjoys full sun or partial shade and moist, well-drained soils. Use it at the front of your borders, in a raised bed or in containers to create an early splash of colour. H and S 15cm (6in).

- Tip - soak the tubers in water overnight prior to planting.

My Mum

Above: Angela with her mother, in 1942
Left: Angela today

Every Friday evening my sister Judith and I would sit on the rug in front of the fire while Mum patiently pressed waves into our very straight, just-washed hair. Whoever was having their hair done would sit up against her knees.

She would ask us what we had been doing at school and listen to us reading or reciting a poem we had to learn. "If you can say it before you go to bed, you'll be able to say it in the morning," she always said. These were happy 'mother and daughter' times, while Dad would be off for a pint at the local.

It was at my mother's knee that we learnt the facts of life when Mum was pregnant with my younger sister, Francesca. We were allowed to place our hands on her tummy and feel the baby kick. It made us feel especially close to her and the baby she carried.

Mrs Angela Wilson, South Ruislip

A RECIPE FOR YOU

Roast Lamb with Orange and Rosemary
(Serves 4-6)

- I x 1.25 kg (2 ½ lb) lean lamb leg joint
- Grated zest of I orange
- 2 cloves garlic, peeled and sliced, optional
- 3 large sprigs fresh rosemary
- I tablespoon olive oil
- Salt and freshly milled black pepper
- 3 tablespoons orange marmalade
- I tablespoon plain flour
- 150 ml (¼ pint) water
- Juice of I orange

1 Preheat the oven to 180-190°C, 350-375°F, Gas Mark 4-5.
2 Place the lamb on a chopping board and make several slits all over the joint. Mix together the orange zest, garlic, the leaves from 2 rosemary sprigs, (removed from the stalk) and the oil. Season.
3 Stuff the mixture into the slits. Place on a metal rack in a roasting tin and open roast for 25 minutes per 450 g (1 lb) plus 25 minutes for medium, and 30 minutes per 450 g (1 lb) plus 30 minutes for well-done. Continue to baste the joint with the lamb juices. Glaze the joint with the orange marmalade 10-15 minutes before the end of the cooking time.
4 Remove the joint from the oven, wrap loosely in foil and allow to rest for 10-15 minutes.
5 To make the gravy, place the roasting tin on the hob, skim off any surface fat, leaving the lamb juices. Increase the heat and stir in the flour. Add the water and orange juice, bring to the boil, reduce the heat and simmer, stirring occasionally, for about 8 minutes, until thickened and glossy.
6 Pour any lamb juices from the joint into the gravy, season and serve the lamb with the gravy, new or roasted potatoes and seasonal vegetables.

RECIPE COURTESY QUALITY STANDARD BEEF AND LAMB

TOP TIP

Keep a pair of shoes outside a room you are decorating then you'll have something to change into when you leave, to stop you walking paint all over the house
Mrs Margaret Rowling, Newton Aycliffe, County Durham

✚ YOUR GOOD HEALTH ✚

Beat breath problems
Bad breath is usually the result of dental or digestive problems. If your dentist has ruled out the former, improve your digestion by taking a probiotic supplement, and eating plenty of foods that encourage friendly gut bacteria, such as green vegetables and live yoghurt. Take one eighth of a teaspoon of sodium bicarbonate 20 minutes after eating, to create the alkaline environment bacteria flourish in. For instant help, chew parsley – it's a natural breath freshener.

Etiquette for Everybody
– 1920s' style –

On conversation…
'But though the so-called tongue-tied folk are the first to recognise their shortcomings, it never seems to occur to those who talk incessantly that they are unduly tiresome. There is a wide gulf between the brilliant conversationalist and the everlasting talker.'

Plant of the week

Although Corylus avellana 'Contorta', the corkscrew hazel, may ultimately reach 6m (20ft) in height, it will only reach half that in 25 years because it's extremely slow-growing. It looks spectacular during the spring when its curiously contorted stems stand out against a cloudless sky, especially when they're adorned with tassel-like catkins.

● **Tip** – Create an extra season of interest by growing a late-flowering clematis such as C viticella through its branches.

A treasured memento

My memento is not in my home but in my garden.

My husband was disabled for eight years, losing both his legs with diabetes. He knew I didn't like money spent on bouquets of flowers, but loved little plants for the garden or the house. He bought me two bags of daffodil bulbs, then sat in his wheelchair and told me to plant them in the little side lawn.

"There you are. We'll see them each spring to remind us of today." Unfortunately, he died before the spring, but now each spring they burst into bloom and I remember him and that day – and each year they multiply. So that is really special for me.

Mrs Vera Dean, Exeter

And another thing...

The best anti-ageing cream is ice cream. What other food makes you feel eight years old again?   *Anon*

Squashed frogs and strawberries

We lived in the country in the 1920s, and school was more than two miles away at Charing in Kent. Breakfast was porridge or cornflakes, either egg and bacon, or sausages, or herrings or kippers. We took two slices of bread and Marmite for dinnertime, and I'd put my head under the tap for a drink.

The first quarter of a mile to school was up a mud track and as we left at 8am for school at 9am, we'd plenty of time to look for birds' nests in the hedges – and count the squashed frogs and toads in the roads. The steam lorries with the solid tyres were the main culprits!

Pocket money was a Saturday halfpenny for a few weeks, then back to a toffee at bedtime. I have an entry in a 1934 diary, 'Got up at 4am. Picked 60lbs of strawberries in 2 hours for five shillings. Gave Eva 3d, Betty 3d' [my sisters].

Mr L Bell, Maidstone, Kent

The author with his two sisters, Eva and Betty

My Mum

Mum was a good cook and while I like to think she passed many of her cooking tips on to me, I can't make pancakes like she used to.

When my sister and I were small, Shrove Tuesday was always an event in our house – not only because of the quality of the pancakes but because of the quantity!

We'd usually eaten our evening meal before Dad got in at night. He worked in an office in London and the trains were frequently late, so we didn't wait for him, except on pancake night. I can see my mum now, almost tied to the kitchen stove, her face flushed as she mixed up bowlfuls of batter and cooked pancake after pancake for the three of us. Then she'd sprinkle sugar over them before we used our lemons. Eventually she'd get to sit down and have one or two herself.

Last pancake night found me cooking pancakes too but I'm ashamed to say, from a packet of batter mix. Thank goodness Mum couldn't see me doing that after the wonderful pancakes she produced.

Pat today   *Pat Rolfe, Hornchurch*

Plant of the week

The cowslip is one of this country's prettiest spring flowers and loved by naturalists. Commonly seen at the base of hedgerows, its numbers have declined sharply, so we should all add it to our gardens. It produces a rosette of leaves from which a stem emerges, topped with a cluster of nodding, scented yellow flowers. H 25cm (10in).

● **Tip** – Cowslips can be used to make a potent wine, but don't collect them from the wild – it's against the law!

My Prayer

I say this prayer I wrote myself every evening and it gives me strength and guidance to face a new day.
Be with me Lord as I lay my head upon my pillow
Be with me as I waken and walk into the unknown day
Be always with my loved ones and my friends and neighbours, Lord
Take care of our beautiful planet
And as I climb the stairs, may the stars shine down
To guide me, strengthen me, and lead me
To eventual eternal rest with You

Mrs Jackie Sheppard, Bristol

Etiquette for Everybody
– 1920s' style –

On personal cleanliness…
'Correct dress and personal cleanliness go hand-in-hand. Dirty finger nails are not tolerated anywhere but in the workshop.'

A RECIPE FOR YOU

French Lemon Tart
(Serves 10-12)

- 100 g (approx 4 oz) golden icing sugar
- 1 egg
- 1 drop of vanilla extract
- 250 g (approx 9 oz) flour
- 25 g (1 oz) ground almonds
- A pinch of salt
- 150 g (5 oz) butter

For the Filling:
- 3 lemons
- 6 eggs
- 275 g (10 oz) golden caster sugar
- 250 g (9 oz) double cream (semi-whipped)

1 Stir together the golden icing sugar and the egg and add the vanilla.

2 Place the flour, almonds and salt in a bowl and rub in the butter.

3 Add the egg and sugar mixture and mix lightly until it forms a ball. Allow to rest in the fridge for about an hour.

4 Roll out the pastry and line a 28 cm, 2 ½ cm deep, flan tin.

5 Bake 'blind' for 15 minutes at 190°C, 375°F or Gas Mark 5.

For the filling

6 Grate the zest and squeeze the juice from the lemons.

7 Break the eggs into a bowl, add the golden caster sugar and beat lightly until blended.

8 Pour cream onto the egg mixture and stir in the lemon juice and zest.

9 Pour into the pastry case and bake for 40 minutes at 150°C, 300°F, Gas Mark 2.

10 When cold, dust with golden icing sugar and serve.

- This recipe contains nuts

RECIPE COURTESY BILLINGTON'S

Musical Matthew

Matthew, aged about three

This is a photograph of one of my seven grandchildren, Matthew. Didn't he have a cheeky look on his face as we were out walking in Cheshire where he lives.

Now, at 16, he towers over me, very polite and very intelligent. His main interest is the rock band he plays the guitar in – they have done a few 'gigs', as they say. He's also composed a piece of music for one of his exams. And I like it, too!

Mrs D A Lightfoot, Keyworth, Notts

And another thing...

'Ukulele' means 'jumping flea' in Hawaiian, and refers to the fast movement of the player's fingers.

✚YOUR GOOD HEALTH✚

Red in the face?

The skin condition acne rosacea is thought to affect one in 15 of us. Characterised by a permanent flushing of the skin, it can range from mild to severe, and most commonly appears in middle age. Alcohol, caffeine, spicy foods and changes in temperature can trigger attacks, so avoid these, and always wear sunscreen to protect your skin outdoors. Taking a 1000mg supplement of vitamin C could help strengthen the blood vessels of the face.

Wartime memories

Having been evacuated to separate homes, Michael Wood of Fareham and his brother attempted a great escape

Soon after the war started, my brother Peter and I were evacuated from St Leonards-on-Sea in Sussex to Ware in Hertfordshire. We were homed separately and neither of us could settle. Being the elder, I decided that we would run away and get back home, little realising that this was 100 miles or so away.

We both met up and started walking across some fields, not really knowing where we were going. After a fairly short time we came out on a road where I saw a young couple and asked: "Please could you tell me the road to Hastings?"

They had, I remember, a red car with an open top which I think might have been an MG.

Of course, they suspected that we were evacuees. These two kind people must have taken us to the local authorities or WVS and we were eventually put, together, with a lovely elderly couple named Mr and Mrs Robinson.

They had a little fruit and veg shop in the High Street in Stansted Abbots. At the side of the shop there was a yard with a hand water pump – no tap water– and the toilet (just a bucket under a wooden seat) was nearly half way down the garden. There was a river at the bottom of the garden and we used to see frogs and tadpoles.

The garden also contained fruit trees, the produce of which was sold in the shop – apart from the ones we pinched!

Granny, as we called her, used to show us up to bed, carrying an oil lamp. When we woke in the morning, we would look under our pillows and find two biscuits each which she called our 'mornings'. We were taught to say grace before we ate our meals and I remember the Christmas dinner of 1940 when Granddad lit the pudding with brandy – quite exciting at the time!

♻ Keen to be green / Everyday ways to save the planet

- DIY enthusiasts use jam jars for holding nails, screws etc. When the metal lid is attached to the underside of a shelf, the glass jar can easily be unscrewed when its contents are needed. Alternatively, pass clean jam jars on to anyone you know who makes their own jam or keeps bees for honey. WI market stalls are also glad to receive them.

- If you have some hardcore left over from a building project, don't waste it –advertise it free to anyone who is prepared to come and take it away.

- Old toothbrushes are invaluable for a whole range of cleaning jobs, from dusting intricately carved items to scrubbing away the limescale around the base of taps. If the bristles become gummed up with use, just trim the ends off.

- Consider the alternative of using natural, non-toxic paints for decorating. To find out more, contact Auro Organic Paint Supplies (tel: 01452 772020, website: www.auro.co.uk) or Ecospaints (tel: 01524 852 371, website: www.organic-paints.co.uk).

- Spring cleaning often involves brightening things up with a spot of paint but what do you do with the bit that's left in the can? Some parts of the country have a RePaint scheme (website: www.communityrepaint.org.uk) but if it doesn't operate in your area, there may be a local amateur dramatic society that can use it for painting scenery.

In the garden

- Empty yoghurt cartons can be used for starting off seeds or, sunk in the ground, as containers for beer to act as a slug-trap.

Quiz

Test your knowledge with this fun quiz. If you get stuck the answers are at the bottom of the page.

PIC: REX FEATURES

1 Which king, according to legend, tried to command the incoming tide?

2 Which is the first London train station you come to as you go around the board in the game of Monopoly?

3 Which actor starred alongside Celia Johnson in the 1945 film, Brief Encounter?

4 Which group won the Eurovision Song Contest in 1976 with the song, Save All Your Kisses For Me?

5 If you suffered from chorophobia, what would you have a fear of?

6 Which host appeared alongside Muffin The Mule on British television from 1946 until 1955?

7 When did Queen Elizabeth II celebrate her silver jubilee?

8 What word in the phonetic alphabet represents the letter J?

9 Daley Thompson won a gold medal at the Moscow Olympics in 1980 and the Los Angles Olympics in 1984. But in which event did he triumph?

10 Who is Superman's journalistic alter ego?

11 In what year was Dick Barton Special Agent first heard over the radio airwaves of the BBC?

12 The acronym CIA represents the name of which American organisation?

1 King Canute
2 Fenchurch Street
3 Trevor Howard
4 Brotherhood Of Man
5 Dancing
6 Annette Mills
7 1977
8 Juliet
9 Decathlon
10 Clark Kent
11 1946
12 Central Intelligence Agency

Dean Cain as Superman but what was his alter ego called?

Keep on running

by Caroline Michel

Mick had agreed to run the London marathon but his heart wasn't in the race

Looking around him, Mick saw the field had thinned out since the start of the race, but only because everyone was passing him. He was losing speed and he knew it.

'Why on earth did I enter?' he wondered as he continued to jog. His heart wasn't in it when he'd filled in the form and it wasn't in it now. He'd been persuaded by some of his mates down at the pub who'd said he couldn't refuse helping Cancer Research.

"You used to run a bit, didn't you, Mick?" Bob had said. "You're our best hope."

"Used to run a bit!" he smiled wanly to himself, "You could say that." He'd been a budding David Bedford in his time. He had represented his county in his youth, and was even picked for England, although he'd had to pull out with a hamstring injury. That had ended his competitive career but it seemed a natural progression to turn to marathon running. He'd done well, raising thousands for various charities over the years. But that was before he'd lost Annie.

His face clouded as he thought of his beautiful Annie. They'd met in the sixth form and married within two years of leaving school. Three bouncing babies followed. But what he recalled now was those months watching her fade away, her face contorted with pain and her large, brown eyes beseeching him to help her. There was nothing he could do, apart from making her as comfortable as he could and doling out pain relief as often as he dared.

'If only I could take the pain for her,' he'd thought, holding her in his arms. Eventually he'd had to let her go. Throughout the whole nightmare, the kids had been brilliant – shopping, cleaning, ironing, arranging the funeral and supporting him the whole time. Even now, one or other of them popped in every day to see him or telephoned to see how he was.

His employers had been great, too, allowing him all the time he'd needed to nurse Annie and afterwards, to recover – if recovery was the right word. He managed to get up each day, eat food and stare blankly at the television. Was that recovery? After a couple of weeks he had gone back to work, and the familiar routine helped a bit. Then, without warning, he'd simply fallen apart.

Mick Chivers, aged 63, retired due to ill health. That was 'company speak' for 'can't hack it any more'. Some days he stayed in his pyjamas; no point in getting washed or dressed. He knew the kids worried, but he didn't care.

His steps faltered and, lifting his arm to wipe the sweat from his brow, he took a brief break. The familiar landmarks, even London Bridge, had failed to register. He took a bottle of water from an outstretched hand, and after taking a few gulps, emptied the rest over his burning head. He was nearing that point where the pain became unbearable, where his legs felt unable to carry on. In the past he'd sailed through this barrier with no problems. But that was before.

His skull felt as though a metal helmet was pressing down on it. He didn't care whether he completed the race or not. He hadn't prepared

> But what he recalled now was those months watching her fade away

PIC: REX FEATURES

Embankment, music was playing. 'Dum da dum', he recognised the song as it penetrated the gloom in his brain. "Keep on running," that was it, "Keep on running," The tears flowed freely, mingling with the salty sweat pouring down his face and neck.

In the old days, Annie had gone with him on his practice runs. Holding the stopwatch, she'd wobbled along beside him on her old bike, sometimes holding a radio so he could reach a steady rhythm, sometimes singing herself. "Keep on runnin'," she'd sung, "Keep on hidin', one fine day I'm gonna be the one to make you understand. Oh yeah, I'm gonna be your man." They had laughed together at the words. His pace quickened as he started to run in time to the familiar tune, his feet felt lighter.

A grin spread across his face as he felt the blood coursing through his veins. He'd got his second wind and was beginning to catch up with the stragglers. People were waving at him, urging him on; he waved back. "One fine day I'm gonna be the one to make you understand." He was actually passing runners now, striding out like he used to do, running for Annie.

He knew he was going to make it. He could see the finishing line, the ribbon stretched across the Mall. As he got nearer he could see Annie's lovely face, her eyes sparkling with joy at his achievement.

He blinked and wiped his eyes – was he hallucinating? No, there she was, high above the crowds. It was a photo he had taken when they were on holiday blown up, poster-size, and held aloft. As he reached the ribbon, he saw his children and grandchildren cheering and waving, holding up the poster.

He was whistling as he turned the key in his door that evening and glanced round the garden. 'I'll plant some pansies this weekend,' he thought, as he went inside, 'they were her favourites.'

properly for it. He'd done a few training runs but turned for home long before he had reached his target distance.

His eye was caught by the profusion of daffodils in parks and window-boxes and he thought he really ought to get out in the garden and do some planting. Tears sprang to his eyes as he remembered how much Annie had loved their garden.

On he plodded, slower and slower, thinking that perhaps he'd call it a day. Along the Victoria

April 2006

Saturday

1

April Fool's Day

Sunday

2

Monday

3

Tuesday

4

Wednesday

5

Thursday

6

Grand National Meeting

Friday

7

Grand National Meeting

Saturday

8

Grand National Meeting

Sunday

9

Palm Sunday

Monday

10

Tuesday

11

Wednesday

12

Thursday

13

Friday

14

Good Friday (Bank Holiday)

Saturday

15

Sunday

16

Easter Day

Monday

17

Easter Monday (Bank Holiday, except Scotland)

Tuesday

18

Wednesday

19

Thursday

20

Friday

21

Queen's birthday

Saturday

22

Sunday **23** St George's Day	Thursday **27**
Monday **24**	Friday **28**
Tuesday **25**	Saturday **29**
Wednesday **26** **Yours** April 26 issue on sale	Sunday **30**

Flavour of the month

April, with its tender green leaves and delicate blossoms, has been described as 'the angel of the months'. At last we feel that spring is truly here and Easter, with its glad message of resurrection, feels especially joyful when it falls in April, as it does this year.

Perhaps for the first time since Christmas, families get together over the Easter weekend. While the children have fun searching for hidden Easter eggs, their parents and grandparents exchange gifts of chocolates and bunches of spring flowers. And everyone sits down together for a delicious Sunday lunch of roast lamb with all the trimmings.

William Shakespeare was born on the 23rd (St George's Day) so perhaps he was ruefully recalling a few birthdays spoiled by April showers when he wrote:
'The uncertain glory of an April day,
Which now shows all the beauty of the sun,
And by and by a cloud takes all away!'

But the unpredictable weather won't keep gardeners indoors at a time of the year when there are a thousand and one jobs to be done, from pricking out seeds to weeding. If you are not too sure of the right time to set your potatoes, listen carefully and take heed of the old saying: 'When you hear the cuckoo shout, 'tis time to plant your tatties out.'

Even those of us who don't know the difference between a dead heat and a blanket finish like to have a flutter on the Grand National at Aintree April 8 – no wonder the bookies call this race the housewives' favourite.

PIC: ANN PICKFORD/REX FEATURES

My Mum

In 2002, after amicably separating from my husband, I moved into a rented house with my five-year-old son – an upheaval – but Mum was there to help and reassure my son, Alex, that he was loved and cherished and this move was an adventure in itself.

Six weeks later I was diagnosed with breast cancer and could not continue in employment, thereby losing my income, company car and general enthusiasm for life.

Mum was with me all through my eight weeks of chemotherapy, surgery and radiotherapy, as well as taking my son to school every day.

I have been blessed with the most wonderful Mum, grandmother, confidante, counsellor, and best friend anyone could imagine, and would certainly endorse the cliché that there are angels on Earth – we have one of our very own.

Ms Julie Harrod,
Grantham

A treasured memento

When I first left home at 16 years old to earn a little to ease things at home in a big family, I saved my pennies for a long time until I had six shillings. Then I bought a brooch for my mum – it was a cameo of a mother with a small child on her lap – it was so evocative. She wore it on her coat lapel all the time, and after we lost her I asked my dear dad if I could have it – it is my most treasured memento.

Mrs Beryl Godsland,
Stamford, Lincolnshire

Great Grandma Beryl on her scooter in the garden, which was a surprise present from her elder son on her 88th birthday

Etiquette for Everybody
– 1920s' style –
On letter writing…
'Stick the stamp on straight. The so-called language of stamps can be summed up in two words – bad taste.'

TOP TIP
Shaving cream is a great instant spot remover if you have no carpet cleaner available. It's particularly effective on makeup, lipstick, coffee and tea. Work it well into the stain and rinse with cold water or soda water.

And another thing...
The course of true love
Early stages: *'Darling, you look so frail and feminine in that dress.'*
Closing stages: *'Help me move this sofa, will you?'*

✚YOUR GOOD HEALTH✚
Freshen the air
We all like our homes to smell clean and fragrant, but an American study found the synthetic musks in air fresheners could suppress your immune system. So perfume your home with natural essential oils instead – try putting three drops each of bergamot, rosewood, geranium and grapefruit oils into a diffuser or oil burner. They all have uplifting properties to boost your mood, too!

Plant of the week

Sweet violets, or Viola odorata, are most at home in the dappled shade of woodland, so use them beneath trees to create a tapestry of colour with other spring flowers. They self-seed freely and make great ground cover. Propagation is easiest by division so break off a small section with roots, pot it up until it has established and then plant it out. H8cm (3in).

- **Tip** – The edible leaves can be harvested all year round, the edible flowers in late winter and early spring.

My Prayer

In Remembrance
This prayer is just lest we forget
The passing on of our dear pets,
Remember too – the waifs and strays
Who've not known love for all their days.
Those abused, abandoned too
The beaten – still forever true
The cowed, the lost, unwanted hounds
Awaiting life, or death, in pounds.
Our hearts go out to every one
From loved and true companions...
To those who crave an owner's touch
And need our love so very much.
And as we speak these heartfelt words
Please God, just let our prayer be heard.
                                Judy Zatonski

A RECIPE FOR YOU

Pork Jambalaya
(Serves 4)

- 15 ml (1 tablespoon) oil
- 1 onion, chopped
- 2 cloves garlic, crushed
- 4 thick spicy sausages
- 450 g (approx 1 lb) lean pork fillet, cut into 1.25 cm (½ inch) cubes
- 30 ml (2 tbsp) jerk seasoning
- 225 g (8 oz) long grain rice
- 397 g (approx) can chopped tomatoes
- 600 ml (approx 1 pt) stock
- 15 ml (1 tablespoon) tomato purée
- ½ red pepper, seeded and cut into small cubes
- ½ yellow pepper, seeded and cut into small cubes
- 5 spring onions, sliced
- 1 chilli (optional)
- 30 ml (2 tablespoons) fresh coriander, chopped

1 Heat the oil in a large saucepan, then add the onion and garlic and cook for 2 minutes until softened.
2 Add the sausages and cook until brown, then remove the sausages and cool slightly, then chop each into three pieces.
3 Add the chopped pork fillet, and cook until browned. Add the jerk seasoning and cook for a further minute.
4 Add the rice and stir until coated in the spices. Pour in the can of chopped tomatoes, then add the stock, tomato purée, and the red and yellow peppers.
5 Return sausages to the pan and stir well, cover and simmer for 30 minutes, stirring occasionally (you may need to add extra liquid if the mixture is sticky).
6 Cook uncovered for a further 10-15 minutes until thickened, then add the spring onions, the chilli, and the fresh coriander.
7 Serve with crusty bread and extra steamed vegetables.

RECIPE COURTESY OF THE BRITISH MEAT INFORMATION SERVICE

TOP TIP

My eyesight is not as good as it used to be – I always used to be losing my hairnet, but now I pop mine in a brightly coloured tin. It is easily seen in my drawers among my other bits and bobs

Mrs Emily Turton, Widnes

A treasured memento

My favourite memento is a 10 carat gold locket given to me by my Godmother as a christening present, which I have now had for 76 years.

Miss June V Bishop, Romford

June in her grandmother's arms

Plant of the week

Muscari, the grape hyacinth, is worth a place in every garden because of the intense purple-blue flowers it produces during spring. A vigorous and sometimes thug-like bulbous perennial, it can become invasive if planted in your borders so is best grown in a container. Move it to the front of your display when in flower, then to a shady corner as the flowers fade and the bulbs take nutrients back from the leaves. H20cm (8in).
● **Tip** – If you have plenty of space, let muscari naturalise in grass

My Prayer

I found this prayer in the information booklet of a hotel. Since then, I say it daily, when I wake.
Thank you God, for all you have given us in this world
For all the beauty and good things we enjoy
But most of all, the promise of eternal life
Please help me to share these blessings with others.
Mrs Shirley Wilkinson, Horncastle

Etiquette for Everybody
– 1920s' style –

On husbands…
'Most husbands have a great deal for which to thank their wives. They should show their appreciation tangibly, and not take it for granted that their wives know of their feeling of indebtedness.'

And another thing...

'Women are around all the time, but World Cups come only every four years.'
Peter Osgood, footballer

Orange Scented Crème Caramel
(Serves 4)

- 450 ml (³/₄ pt) skimmed milk
- 75 g (3 oz) granulated cane sugar
- Zest and juice of 1 large orange
- 1 teaspoon coriander seeds, lightly crushed
- 3 medium eggs

1 Heat the milk with 1 tablespoon of the granulated cane sugar, orange zest and coriander seeds until almost boiling. Set aside for 20 minutes for the flavours to develop.
2 Meanwhile, place the remaining sugar in a heavy-based pan and cook over a gentle heat for 1-2 minutes, shaking the pan occasionally until all the sugar has melted, then caramelised. Remove from the heat and pour in 2 tablespoons of the orange juice – careful as the mixture will splatter – and stir until a smooth sauce forms. Divide the sauce between four 150 ml (¹/₄ pt) ramekin dishes.
3 Preheat the oven to 170°C, 325°F, Gas Mark 3. Beat the eggs, then strain over the warm milk, discarding the zest and seeds. Mix the eggs and milk well, then pour into the ramekin dishes.
4 Place the ramekins in a large roasting tin and pour hot water from the kettle to come halfway up the outside of the dishes.
5 Bake for 25-30 mins or until the custards are set in the middle. Remove from the tin and leave to cool. Chill for at least 1 hour.
6 To serve, invert the crème caramels onto plates and top with spun sugar, if desired.

RECIPE COURTESY TATE & LYLE

A visit to Grandma

Rosalie Armitage from Aberdeen wrote a poem about her Grandma's house, and here is an extract:

A visit to Grandma was a thing of great joy,
I would rather have that than any new toy,
The memories I have of those days long ago
Well, I'll write you a 'picture' and then you will know.

The old garden door so tall and so strong,
The walls so high and the blackbird's song
In the apple trees, the wild privet hedge
And old lace brushing the wash kitchen ledge.

I'll tell you some more, though, if you care to hear,
In the old summer house we played year after year.
We had boxes for chairs and a table of wood
And leaves and rose petals mixed up for food.

The lawn was so long it felt miles to run down
Till we got to the sun dial just placed like a crown
It seemed as if it had the best view of all,
Of marigolds, roses and delphiniums tall.

We would sit in a room full of beauty and age,
And she'd tell us her tales as though read from a page.
Yes, my Grandma, her house and the family around her
Are my most precious memories; without I'd be poorer.

✚YOUR GOOD HEALTH✚

Get fit for spring
The lighter mornings should leave you feeling more energetic, so make the most of it by getting some exercise. Swimming and aqua aerobics are great for toning your muscles and boosting overall fitness without putting pressure on your joints, says the Arthritis Research Campaign. For more information on joint-friendly fitness, including a booklet on the best exercise for back pain, call 01246 558033 or visit the website www.arc.org.uk

A RECIPE FOR YOU

Chicken on Wilted Watercress Pappardelle
(Serves 4)

- 1 tablespoon olive oil
- 4 chicken breast fillets
- 100 ml (4 fl oz) red wine or stock
- 1 x 350 g (12 oz) jar tomato and chilli pasta sauce
- 225 g (8 oz) pappardelle pasta ribbons
- 1 x 85 g (approx 3½ oz) bag watercress
- ¼ teaspoon freshly grated nutmeg
- 25 g (1 oz) Parmesan cheese, sliced

1 Heat 1 teaspoon of the oil in a large non-stick frying pan, add the chicken breasts and fry for 8-10 minutes, turning once until browned on both sides. Add the wine (or stock) and simmer for 2-3 minutes until nearly all evaporated. Add the tomato sauce, cover and simmer for 5 minutes or until the chicken is very nearly cooked through.
2 Meanwhile, cook the pasta in a large pan of boiling salted water for 7 minutes or according to packet instructions until pasta is just tender. Drain in a colander.
3 Place the watercress, nutmeg and remaining oil in the pan, add the pasta and toss to mix, season well with black pepper. Keep warm.
4 Arrange the slices of Parmesan cheese on top of the chicken and place the frying pan under a hot grill. Cook for 2 minutes until the cheese is golden brown. Serve the chicken and sauce on top of the wilted watercress pappardelle.

RECIPE COURTESY THE FRESH CUT STIR FRY ALLIANCE

A very special wedding

I was nursing from 1939 to 1946, when I was married. My husband-to-be was a patient when I was working at a Naval Hospital near Glasgow in 1942, our best man had also been a patient.

Another patient 'gave me away' and a patient's wife made my wedding bouquet of red roses and lily-of-the-valley. The ingredients for our two-tier wedding cake were provided by the patient, and another patient's wife made it.

Despite my lack of family, all my new husband's family, Matron, the doctors and the hospital staff came to my wedding. Sadly, some of these dear people are no longer with us – including my husband, but to those who are, I shall always be eternally grateful for giving me such a wonderful day to remember.

Dot Saintey, Buxton, Derbys

Dot on her wedding day

✚ YOUR GOOD HEALTH ✚

Nail it!

Have a look at your nails – they can tell you quite a bit about your health:

- White spots – a sign you're deficient in the mineral zinc, according to Chinese medicine, so up your intake of eggs, turkey and seafood.
- Horizontal ridges – you're not getting enough B vitamins, so eat more whole grains and chicken.
- Weak, splitting nails – your diet may be low in protein. Include more lean meat, fish, nuts and seeds.

Plant of the week

Fritillaria persica 'Adiyaman' is an unusual-looking plant from Persia with nodding bell-shaped flowers of the deepest purple. If planted in large groups it will add drama to your borders during the spring, and may reach 1.5m (5ft) in height. It thrives in well-drained soil in a sunny position.

- **Tip** – Accentuate the purple colour scheme by underplanting it with purple heuchera and perilla.

Etiquette for Everybody
- 1920's style -

On wives...
'The average woman thrives on affection. Do not starve your wife in this direction.'

My Mum

Above: Violet's toys sitting on the sofa
Inset: Shirley and Violet pretty in lilac and pink at a wedding

At the age of 42 I was diagnosed with rheumatoid arthritis and after a few years I joined the local branch of the Arthritis and Rheumatism Council for Research, and began raising money for them.

My Mum, Violet, wanted to help too, and after some thought she decided that she would knit toys to sell. She'd knitted the odd baby coat and bootees but had never knitted toys. Well, hers were brilliant. They sold very well and made hundreds of pounds for ARC!

She died ten years ago, at the age of 82. She was a gentle soul and I still miss her and our afternoons spent knitting.

Mrs Shirley Rhyder, Bovey Tracey, Devon

And another thing...

'Waiter, there's a fly in my soup!'
1 'It's okay, he'll sink when he's dead'
2 'I'll get him a spoon.'
3 'Oh dear, are you a vegetarian?'
4 'Just be grateful it wasn't a 'hare.'

✚ YOUR GOOD HEALTH ✚

Tackle piles

Piles are a type of varicose vein in the rectum. They're very common in older people, especially if you're frequently constipated. Ease them by taking 500mg of the bioflavonoid rutin three times daily – it helps strengthen blood vessels, and you can find it in your local health food store. Make sure your diet's high in fibre, too – oats, wholegrain bread, and fruit and vegetables are excellent sources.

A treasured memento

This is my memento – a picture of the Queen taken in 1999 when she came with Prince Philip to open our Triangle Leisure Centre. The bunch of tulips she is holding was given to her by my granddaughter, Louise, then aged 6.

Evelyn Payne, A smiling Queen carrying
West Sussex Louise's tulips

My Prayer

An extract from:
A Farming Hymn
Thank you Lord, for this, our country
Fields of brown and gold and green
Without these there'd be no living
There would be no crops to glean.
Very often things don't work out
As we wish that it should be
But the Lord has planned before us
It will work, I'm sure you'll see

Thank you Lord, for windy weather
Drying out the Winter's gloom
Sunshine mixed with April showers
Causing everything to bloom.
All the work is done in seasons
Everything will grow in turn
Watch for different pictures daily
Something new to see and learn

Thank you Lord, for sending people
Who can work and till the ground
Giving yet another harvest
All to help the world around.
Thank you Lord, for being near us
Watching everything we do
Blessing all our homes and farmland
Seeing all our seasons through
Betty Alcock, Brixworth, Northampton

A RECIPE FOR YOU

Apricot and Cardamom Muffins
(Makes 6-8)

● 8-10 cardamom pods
● 225 g (8 oz) plain white flour
● 2 teaspoons baking powder
● 50 g (2 oz) light brown soft sugar
● 75 g (3 oz) ready to-eat dried apricots finely chopped
● 100 g (4 oz) butter, melted
● 2 medium eggs, beaten
● 150 ml (¼ pt) low-fat natural yoghurt
● 2 teaspoons demerara sugar

1 Preheat oven to 200°C, 400°F, Gas Mark 6, 15 minutes before baking. Line the muffin tins with paper cases. Crack the cardamom pods, discard pods, reserving seeds.
2 Sift the flour and baking powder into a mixing bowl, then stir in the light brown soft sugar, chopped apricots and cardamom seeds.
3 Stir in the melted butter, then the eggs and finally the yoghurt. Stir lightly then spoon into the paper cases.
4 Bake in the preheated oven for 20 minutes or until well risen and golden.
RECIPE COURTESY TATE & LYLE

Time Well Spent

Muriel and her brother on the beach at Blackpool in 1938

Long ago when girls and boys
Used their imaginations to play with toys,
No computers, television, compact discs
But soldiers, forts and building bricks.
Into battle the soldiers went
Then returned to their box, a day well spent.

There were three-wheeler bikes and roller skates,
Whips and tops with coloured shapes,
Hopscotch with an empty tin,
Cherry Blossom polish it used to have in.
Rounders, Queenie-o-coco, hide and seek
It didn't cost money, or need any cheek!

A penny we received for our 'spends'
On sweets – the variety was no end –
Gobstoppers, blackjacks, a great lucky bag,
And if you were lucky, ice cream off your dad.

With all of this we were content,
Respected people wherever we went
Even the war did not make us wild
I hope that I was a well-behaved child!

Muriel Clark, Manchester

TOP TIP

An aspirin tablet dissolved in a vase filled with water will revive tired flowers
Mrs A Chambers, Hammersmith

Plant of the week

Dicentra spectabilis produces arching sprays of dainty, rose pink, heart-shaped flowers against a pretty backdrop of green leaves. A favourite of the Victorians, it's graceful, long-flowering and most at home in an herbaceous border. It's simple to grow and thrives in moist soil in sun or partial shade. Lift and divide large clumps during late autumn when the leaves have died down, taking care not to damage the roots. H1.1m.

● **Tip** – Protect young plants from slugs and snails.

Etiquette for Everybody
– 1920s' style –

On shaking hands…
'The chief point lies in grasping the other person's hand with just sufficient strength to express friendliness. A flabby touch suggests that the individual is either cool in his friendship or is one who needs more backbone. On the contrary, the person with a Herculean grip, who thereby forces a lady's rings into her flesh, is voted, on all sides, a nuisance.'

Wartime memories

As a boy, Sid Wright of London cycled around the bomb damaged streets of Westminster delivering newspapers

I lived in Purbeck Place, Westminster through the Blitz in 1940. I was 13 years old and had an early morning paper round. I worked for a lovely chap called Jack Masters who had a paper stall on the corner of Erasmus Street and employed three lads as paper boys.

My widowed mother, who worked as a cleaner in the local government offices, purchased an old telegram boy's bike from the GPO for five shillings. I carried two big bags of daily newspapers and magazines. Jack always said: "Take care; if any of the houses or flats have been hit or damaged during the night or there are UXB bombs, leave them and I will check later." UXBs were unexploded bombs and the streets where they had fallen were usually roped off by the police.

I started at about seven o' clock in the morning. On most days, the all-clear sirens went off around 4am or 5am, occasionally a little later. One good thing about being early, you had the first chance to collect up any souvenirs like bits of shrapnel or shell nose caps from the nightly ack-ack guns. Also incendiary bomb fins after the incendiary had burnt out – there were always plenty of those lying around – but before we picked them up we doused them with a sandbag or water. Later in the war, they put explosives in the fins but, as schoolboys, we didn't fully realise how dangerous they were. I had a cupboard full of these souvenirs!

I continued my paper round until I was 14 years old when I started work as an apprentice electrician. I was also a boy scout and when I was 16, I worked at weekends as a volunteer stretcher bearer at Westminster Hospital. We slept Friday, Saturday and Sunday nights on the vacated fifth floor and when we heard the sirens we went down to the entrance to take people from the ambulances to the main hall where they were attended by the medical staff. Patients with relatively minor injuries were treated there and then before being admitted to one of the wards but those who were in need of urgent attention were taken directly to the operating theatre.

Keen to be green
Everyday ways to save the planet

- Some waste prevention ideas are very, very simple – such as writing on both sides of a sheet of paper!

- Scrunched up plastic carrier bags can be used as a substitute for bubble wrap when packing fragile items.

- Don't be tempted to chuck out aluminium cans to save the bother of rinsing them out because aluminium is one of the most cost-effective materials to recycle and is used to manufacture everything from bikes to satellite dishes.

- Newspapers are great for cleaning windows. Use them dipped in warm water for washing, then polish with dry newspapers to give them a professional sparkle.

- If you put a piece of paper or cardboard on the floor, does your cat immediately go and sit on it? Take the hint and use torn up cardboard and newspaper to make disposable bedding for your pets.

- A pressure cooker is more economical on fuel than conventional cooking methods – and it is perfect for making a delicious stew.

- Use left-over wallpaper for lining drawers and shelves.

In the garden
- Newspapers also make a good cover for plants if a frost is forecast.

Quiz

Test your knowledge with this fun quiz. If you get stuck the answers are at the bottom of the page.

PIC: REX FEATURES

1 From which English port did the Pilgrim Fathers set sail to America?

2 In Greek mythology, who flew too close to the sun?

3 Whose image was used on the 'Your Country Needs You' recruitment posters initially used in the First World War?

4 In Charles Dickens' story, Oliver Twist, what is the name of Bill Sikes' dog?

5 What is Elton John's real name?

6 Ned Kelly was an infamous outlaw from which country?

7 The Chair is an obstacle in which famous race?

8 Which band sung House Of The Rising Sun in 1964?

9 Who wrote Lady Chatterley's Lover?

10 Friday's child is what?

11 What date is St Swithin's Day?

12 In what street did the Great Fire of London start?

1 Plymouth
2 Icarus
3 Lord Kitchener
4 Bullseye
5 Reginald Dwight
6 Australia
7 The Grand National
8 The Animals
9 DH Lawrence
10 Loving and giving
11 July 15
12 Pudding Lane

Pink Snow by Angela Pickering

Mary and John have found contentment late in life but Mary believes there is something vital missing from their home

A sudden breeze wafted through the garden causing blossom to shower down on John and Davie where they sat under the cherry tree. The petals fell softly like pink snowflakes. The child was captivated and jumped to his feet to caper in the soft drift. John watched him and then, surrendering to impulse, he moved stiff limbs and danced beside the boy.

Davie looked up at him: "You look like a dancing, pink snowman," he said. John laughed and brushed petals from the boy's hair. "I'm too old and fat to dance for long," he puffed and retired to the bench while Davie threw handfuls of petals into the air.

John's mind slipped back to the last time he had sat beneath the falling cherry blossom when he had gone there to think after Mary had sprung her 'wonderful' idea on him. He remembered his reaction: "Adopt? At our age? You must be mad, woman. They'd never allow it – and quite rightly, too!"

But Mary had laughed fondly at him. "No, you silly old fool," she replied. "Not a child, a whole family. They adopt us. It's called Adopt a Granny. Though, in our case, it would be granny and granddad."

"You're completely mad, woman," he repeated.

"No John, I'm not going to let you talk me out of this. I want a family and I'm going to have one, whatever you say." He had been dumbfounded. Never in ten years of married life had she stood up to him like that. What had come over her?

She had tried to explain: "You know I always wanted children but I never met the right man, until you." Her smile was a little sad. "And then, of course, it was too late." The expression on his face had touched her and she hurried on, "I've been so happy with you, John. We've had a wonderful time together, just the two of us, but now…" her voice had tailed off, her expression wistful.

"But now, what?"

"Now, I need more. I'm sorry, that's all there is to it."

There was no going back; Mary had arranged everything. These strangers, the young parents and their three (yes, three!) offspring, were coming to meet him. Mary had already charmed them all

and now it was up to him, either to be a part of the new family or be excluded.

Mary smiled: "I'm so excited - you'll love them, John, I know you will."

"I don't like children," he said, making one last appeal for mercy, but knowing there was to be none. "Still, I'll try, for your sake."

"That's all I ask." She touched his shoulder, as if she knew what he was going through. She didn't, of course. How could she? Oh, she knew what he had told her of his short, ill-fated marriage, and the pain of losing both his young wife and the baby that struggled to be born. But after he had told Mary the bare facts, John had always avoided the subject.

Now she wanted him to accept children in his life. "Maybe we're too set in our ways, Mary," he'd cautioned. "Children take a lot of effort. Aren't we too old to start something like this?" Mary had dismissed his concerns with a wave of her hand. "There are two little girls, twins, and a boy," she'd said. "You can teach him to fish. I can teach them to cook. Their parents both have to work full-time." She paused and laid a hand on his shoulder. "They need us, John."

He had retreated, sighing, to his favourite bench under the cherry tree. He wished that he

"Adopt? At our age? You must be mad woman. They'd never allow it"

could stay hidden there until this crisis was over but Mary appeared before him. "You're covered in petals," she laughed. "The blossom doesn't last very long, does it?'

He closed his eyes for a moment and said: "I sometimes think that beauty has to be fleeting. If it lasts too long, we get used to it and can't see the wonder any more."

"Oh no," she shook her head. "That oak tree is every bit as lovely as the cherry, it just takes longer to appreciate, that's all."

John stood up, brushing the petals onto the grass. In a sudden moment of clarity, he took her hand and raised it to his lips. Blinking furiously to dispel the tears which suddenly filled his eyes, he whispered against her fingers: "Oh, Mary,

how have you put up with me all this time?"

"Some things are worth waiting for," she said, "like the oak." They had wandered down the garden to stand hand in hand under the spreading branches of the old tree, a new understanding growing between them. John broke the silence: "Mary, do you think we should tie an old car tyre on this branch here? It'd make a grand swing for the children when they visit."

A shriek of delight brought John tumbling back to the present. Two small girls came flying down the path to join their brother in the flower-fight. The air was filled with pink snow again. The smell of freshly baked cakes drifted from the kitchen. Mary joined him on the bench and they sat watching as the children played.

"No regrets?" whispered Mary.

John knew that a squeeze of her hand was all the answer she needed. This last year had been full of wonder for them both: a time of slowly getting to know the children and their parents, of accepting them into their lives, and building new relationships.

Davie climbed onto John's knee and rested his head against John's tweedy shoulder. "Will this happen every year?" he asked.

"Oh yes, Davie, my boy," replied John. "Sure as eggs is eggs."

Davie chuckled at the odd saying, as John knew he would. Then, gazing up into John's eyes, he said the words that would seal their relationship forever: "Will you push me on the tyre swing, Granddad?"

May 2006

Monday

1   May Day Bank Holiday

Tuesday

2

Wednesday

3

Thursday

4

Friday

5

Saturday

6

Sunday

7

Monday

8

Tuesday

9

Wednesday

10

Thursday

11

Friday

12

Saturday

13

Sunday

14

Monday

15

Tuesday

16

Wednesday

17

Thursday

18

Friday

19

Saturday

20

Sunday

21

Monday

22

Tuesday	Sunday
23 Chelsea Flower Show (provisional)	**28**
Wednesday	Monday
24 **Yours** May 24 issue on sale Chelsea Flower Show (provisional)	**29** Spring Bank Holiday
Thursday	Tuesday
25 Chelsea Flower Show (provisional)	**30**
Friday	Wednesday
26 Chelsea Flower Show (provisional)	**31**
Saturday	
27 Chelsea Flower Show (provisional)	

PIC: RESO/REX FEATURES

Flavour of the month

Hooray, it's May! This is the month that gladdens our hearts with sunshine and flowers and the promise of much more to come. In the orchard it is heavenly apple blossom time and in fields and hedgerows one of our loveliest native trees, the horse chestnut, lives up to its other name, the candle-tree.

How fortunate that May has not one, but two, Bank Holidays, giving us extra leisure time to enjoy its delights. In some villages, young girls still dance with ribbons around the maypole on the first of the month, keeping alive a tradition that goes back to pagan times when the rites of spring were celebrated in this way.

Blue skies and longer days make it tempting to throw caution to the winds but beware – frosty nights are still a risk. There is much common sense in the old saying 'Don't cast a clout till May is out', and if you are wise you won't store your woollies away in mothballs just yet.

Similarly, wise gardeners resist the temptation to put out hanging baskets or plant out tender bedding plants until the very end of the month. Keep an eye on the weather forecast and if a sudden drop in temperature is predicted, protect vulnerable shrubs by throwing old net curtains over them.

The asparagus season starts in May and, as it has to be harvested by Midsummer's Day, we have only a short season to enjoy this delicacy. Freshly picked 'sparrow grass', simply steamed and eaten with melted butter, is the flavour of the month.

PIC: REX FEATURES

A treasured memento

From a volcanic islet in Thailand I brought back a 4cm pebble before I realised how beautiful it was. It is off-white and porous with thin igneous layers, which look like a trickle of honey wrapped around it, because the porous stone is slightly more worn away than the glass layers.

Mrs A Simon, London

My Mum

I have many memories of my Mother – of her kindness, her sense of fun (a water pistol fight all round the house comes to mind) – but the strongest memory, which defines her caring nature, was in 1935, when my brother and I contracted diphtheria. I don't know if there was any question of our going into hospital, but I doubt if my mother would have agreed to this. She'd already lost one child to pneumonia, and must have been determined to do all that was humanly possible to see us through this dangerous disease.

There was little treatment for this at the time, twice a day nasal douches and gargling, which she saw we two reluctant patients perform.

Above: Joy and her brother John
Above left: Joy's mum

She also tempted our flagging appetites with dainty foods.

We knew she was devoted to our well being as surely as the sun rose each day. There is much I owe to my mother, and although I don't come up to her standard of goodness, I am thankful my daughter has inherited this caring nature.

Mrs Joy King, West Sussex

✚YOUR GOOD HEALTH✚

A taste of honey

If the warmer weather means a runny nose and itchy eyes for you, try spreading locally-produced honey on your toast. Studies have found eating regular dollops of the sweet stuff from your area could help your body get used to the pollens that trigger your hayfever symptoms.

And another thing...

'Very sorry can't come. Lie follows by post.' *Telegram from Lord Charles Beresford (1846-1919) to the Prince of Wales, on being summoned to dine at the 11th hour.*

Etiquette for Everybody
– 1920s' style –

On lifting...

'The menfolk should invariably see to it that the women of the house do not have to lift heavy weights or perform tasks which call for more than ordinary strength. Women are quick to appreciate such little attentions, and the buttons will get sewn on all the quicker.'

Plant of the week

When it comes to groundcover, lamiums, especially those with attractively silvered leaves such as Lamium 'White Nancy', are hard to beat. Semi-evergreen and with a spreading habit, they thrive in moist soil and dappled shade and will quickly fill the gaps at the front of your borders. Divide large clumps in spring. H 10cm.

- **Tip** – Rip out old leaves in spring. New growth will replace them after a week or so.

My Prayer

The Cottage of Content
They call it the Cottage of Content,
I knocked to find out what it meant
For all my life I sought to find
The secret of a quiet mind.

'Come in,' the owner said, 'Come in,
The things you seek are here within.
Love tends the hearth and keeps the blaze
That warms the heart in better days
Hope trims the lamps and keeps them bright
To give a good and kindly light.

Faith keeps her watch in every room
To banish doubt and fear and gloom'
I turned away and, homeward bound,
Went to build my Cottage of Content

Author unknown
R Hunter, Penrith

A RECIPE FOR YOU

Grilled Trout with Garlic and Tarragon Wild Mushrooms
(Serves 4)

- 1 bunch of asparagus
- Salt and ground black pepper
- 4 trout fillets weighing about 175 g (6 oz) each
- 2 tablespoons olive oil
- Juice of 1 lemon
- 50 g (2 oz) butter, softened
- 2 shallots, finely chopped
- 2 cloves garlic, finely sliced into wafers
- 175 g (6 oz) wild or shitake mushrooms
- Sprigs of tarragon
- Lemon wedges to garnish
- Sauté potatoes to accompany

1 Snap the asparagus in half and discard the woody stalk. Cook in boiling salted water for 2 minutes, then drain and refresh under cold running water.

2 Arrange the trout fillets on a baking sheet and season with salt and ground black pepper. Drizzle with olive oil and a squeeze of lemon juice. Cook under a preheated grill for 8-10 minutes, or until the trout is just cooked.

3 Meanwhile, melt the butter and gently cook the chopped shallots until soft but not coloured, add the garlic and cook for a further 20 seconds. Add the mushrooms and asparagus tips and cook, stirring for a further 1-2 minutes. Toss in the tarragon leaves and season well.

4 Serve the trout with the mushroom and asparagus mixture and accompany with sauté potatoes and lemon wedges.

RECIPE COURTESY THE BRITISH TROUT ASSOCIATION

Etiquette for Everybody
– 1920s' style –

On husbands...
'Some husbands forget to extend the little courtesies to their wives which all polite men bestow on womenfolk. Such neglect is deplorable.'

A treasured memento

Rosemary and husband Eric

I have a treasured memento that takes pride of place in my jewellery box, and I wear it on special occasions. My gold crucifix and chain was a bridesmaid's gift from my big sister and her husband. As a 12-year-old I was so excited to be asked to do this privileged job.

There were three bridesmaids to support the bride, all of us wearing our crucifix necklaces. The weather was mixed, from hot sunshine to hail, which hammered off the corrugated metal of the reception hall! That was 45 years ago. Since then, both my daughters have borrowed my special necklace to wear at their weddings.

Mrs Rosemary Medland, Letchworth

TOP TIP

Keep a pad and pen on your bedside table – so handy in the night for jotting down a great idea, or something you need to add to your shopping list.

Plant of the week

Auriculas are a striking type of primula, with flowers in beautiful, contrasting colours. Essentially man-made, the many hybrids now available will tempt even non-gardeners into giving them a try – once you've grown one, you'll soon become addicted! The sheer artistry of their flowers just begs that you display them properly. Enthusiasts show them in mini theatres, on painted shelves, and against a black background within a gold frame as a way of highlighting their incredible colours.
● **Tip** – If you want to learn more join the National Auricula and Primula Society.

And another thing...

Five famous writers who were nominated for the Nobel prize – but didn't win it:
Thomas Hardy, Mark Twain, Anton Chekhov, H G Wells, Virginia Woolf.

My Prayer

May the peace of Christ be with you
The Love of Christ surround you
And the joy of Christ fill you
To overflowing

May the grace of Christ shine on you
The words of Christ direct you
And the light of Christ fill you
To overflowing
Rachel Hall-Smith, Cheddleton, Staffs

Raspberry Coconut Slice

- 220 g (approx 8 oz) plain flour
- 150 g (5 oz) unsalted butter
- 25 g (1 oz) ground almonds
- 110 g (approx 4 oz) golden caster sugar

Topping
- 175 g (6 oz) unsalted butter
- 175 g (6 oz) golden caster sugar
- Finely grated zest of 1 small lemon
- 3 large eggs, beaten
- 2 tablespoons plain flour
- 300 g (approx 10 oz) desiccated coconut
- 350 g (approx 12 oz) raspberry jam

1 Preheat the oven to 180°C, 350°F, Gas Mark 4.
2 Sift the flour into a bowl and rub in the butter until the mixture resembles breadcrumbs.
3 Stir in the ground almonds and golden caster sugar. Press the mixture into a 20 x 30 cm (8 x 12 ins) baking tin, lined with non-stick baking paper.
4 Bake for 20-25 minutes until golden. Remove from the oven and leave to cool.
5 Cream the butter and golden caster sugar with the lemon zest until light.
6 Gradually beat in the eggs, followed by the flour and the coconut.
7 Spread the jam evenly over the cooled base. Spoon the coconut mixture on top, spreading evenly.
8 Bake for 30-40 minutes until firm. Cool in the tin, and then cut into fingers.

RECIPE COURTESY BILLINGTON'S

Memories of Mum and Dad

The Dolls' Hospital where a little girl's dream would come true

My Mother, Annie Riemann, started a dolls' hospital in the early 1950s. Eventually, she rented the shop in the photograph, where my father had a workshop in the back room. My father had had a doll-making factory in Copenhagen in the 1940s and 1950s, so he helped my mother to paint and mend some of the dolls.

I'd help her make new clothes for the dolls, as I was studying dress design at Art College. It was an awful lot of fun helping out when the shop got busy near Christmas. There were no Barbies in those days, and so with money being short, a good present for a little girl would be a new outfit for her doll – plus new eye lashes and even a new wig and shoes.

My mother's shop was very well known in the North East and she would get dolls sent from all over – I have such fond memories of it all.

Susan Childs, Winchester, Hampshire

+YOUR GOOD HEALTH+

Flower Power

Flower essences are healing tinctures distilled from different blooms, and are thought to help relieve both physical and emotional conditions. You can find them in health food stores. Try...

- Larch, if you lack confidence and have a fear of failure
- Oak, if you're totally exhausted and lacking energy
- Valerian, if you find it hard to relax.

A RECIPE FOR YOU

Lamb Fajitas with Chunky Yoghurt Dip
(Serves 2)

Chunky yoghurt dip
- 120 g (approx 4¹/₂ oz) pot of natural yogurt
- ¹/₄ cucumber, cut into small chunks
- 2 spring onions, finely sliced
- Chilli powder, pinch
- 5 ml (1 teaspoon) fresh mint, chopped

Lamb Fajitas
- 225 g (8 oz) lean lamb neck fillet or lamb leg steaks
- 10 ml (2 teaspoons) fajita seasoning
- 1 carrot, peeled and grated
- 4 spring onions, roughly sliced
- 1 lemon, juice and rind
- 100 g (4 oz) baby spinach leaves
- 4 flour tortillas

1 For the chunky yoghurt dip, mix together the pot of natural yoghurt with the cucumber, 2 spring onions, chilli powder, and fresh mint.

2 Cut the lean lamb neck fillet (or leg steaks) into thin slices or strips and dry fry in a hot non-stick wok for 5-6 minutes. Add the fajita seasoning and cook for a further 1-2 minutes.

3 Add the carrot, 4 roughly sliced spring onions, and the lemon rind and juice to wok. Remove from heat and stir through the baby spinach leaves. Pile into the tortillas, spoon over a large spoonful of the chunky yoghurt dip, roll up and serve.

RECIPE COURTESY OF THE BRITISH MEAT INFORMATION SERVICE

TOP TIP

Place garlic cloves in a full watering can overnight, then use to water plants. The smell will keep insects at bay
Mrs Margaret Rowling, Newton Aycliffe, County Durham

Etiquette for Everybody
– 1920s' style –

On weddings…
'The number of bridesmaids at a wedding is usually four or six, but one, two, up to 12 is reasonable.'

And another thing...

'When things go wrong, as they sometimes will,
When the road you're trudging seems all uphill,
When care is pressing you down a bit,
Rest, if you must, but don't you quit!'   *Anon*

My Prayer

If

*If you could bottle all the smiles of a day
And use them on the bad times
If you could tie up all the cuddles others give you
Then everything would be just fine.*

*If you could iron out troubles when they beat you
Box all the differences and pack them away
If you could face up to life when others falter
You will know who has shown you the way.*

*If you could take back cross words you say in haste
Before each day is through
If you could trust a little more in the Lord
He's always there to stand by you.*

Mrs Vera Ewers, Kirkheaton, Huddersfield

✚YOUR GOOD HEALTH✚

Cystitis help

This painful inflammation of the bladder or urethra can leave you with symptoms including a burning pain when you pass water. Although women are most commonly affected, especially after the menopause, it can affect men too. Prevent attacks by drinking at least 1.5 litres of water daily, and lean back when you go to the toilet, so your bladder is completely emptied. Drinking a couple of glasses daily of unsweetened cranberry juice is helpful – it contains compounds that stop bacteria sticking to the bladder walls.

Plant of the week

Ajuga is one of the most colourful groundcover plants and thrives in sun or shade, although it does best in moist soils. It's a great choice for groundcover as well as for planting in baskets and containers. There are several varieties to choose from, all with lovely spires of flowers during spring, and many have multi-coloured leaves such Rainbow and Variegat'. Little Court Pink (pictured) has plain leaves but lovely flowers during summer. H15cm (6in).

● Tip – Separate rooted stems in early summer to create new plants.

A treasured memento

Lady-in-waiting Barbara (front)

My treasured memento is this photograph which was taken at Kildare School in Leeds when I was about six years old. I'm the one in the front sitting down and was the lady-in-waiting to the May Queen. The photo was a favourite of my beloved parents William and Lily Jeffrey.

I'm now 71 years old and it seems so long since my days at school – which, of course, it is!

Barbara Finch,
Chapel St Leonards

My Mum

Olga and mum Catherine

My Mother and I lived most of our lives in a village called Great Rollright in Oxfordshire where we were evacuated during the war. My Mother loved to entertain people by playing the piano in pubs in the town. There were many Americans stationed around the area as well.

While playing out with my friends one day in 1944 we saw a US Flying Fortress B17 take the top of the trees off and crash half a mile up the road. I ran and told my mother who jumped on her bicycle, with her Woodbines in her apron pocket, and pedalled round to the crash in the pitch black.

Mum pulled out most of the airmen, each asking for a cigarette before they died, and bandaged them where she could with her pinafore and torn up underslip.

Mum never got any recognition, but she was very brave and was someone very special.

Mrs Olga Tyler, Canvey Island

May 22-28

A treasured memento

My treasured memento is a scarf. My sister Kathleen married a wonderful man – a Scot called John McQueen on April 22, 1944 – and I was astounded and honoured to be asked to be his best man at their wedding. At the tender age of 17, this seemed a great task to me but my nerves were put aside and all went well.

The scarf was a thank-you gift for being John's best man. Unfortunately, owing to the situation at that time (six weeks before D-Day)

Ron, aged 17 in 1944, wearing his Paisley scarf

none of his army pals or family could attend.

The scarf had a Paisley design, the colour of wine with cream motifs, with a long fringe – very fashionable at the time. It's still in excellent condition and I'll never part with it.
Ron Bignell, Hinckley, Leics

A RECIPE FOR YOU

Chicken, Avocado and Vegetable Wraps
(Serves 2)

- 30 ml (2 tablespoons) olive oil
- 1 chicken breast fillet, sliced
- 1 red onion, finely sliced
- 1 x 350 g (12 oz) pack fresh cut mushroom stir-fry
- 2 large tortilla wraps
- ½ ripe avocado, peeled, stoned and sliced
- Handful of fresh coriander
- Thai-style chilli dipping sauce to taste

1 Heat a wok and add 1 tablespoon of the oil, swirl it around, then add the chicken and cook for 4 minutes.
2 Add the onion and stir-fry for 3 minutes until the chicken and onion are golden brown; transfer to a bowl.
3 Place the wok back on the heat, add the remaining oil and mushroom stir-fry and cook over a high heat to soften the vegetables, adding 2 tablespoons hot water to help steam them. Stir in the chicken and season to taste.
4 Lay the wraps on a board and divide the chicken and vegetables between them. Lay some sliced avocado on top, the coriander, then generously drizzle with the chilli sauce. Wrap them up tightly and serve.

RECIPE COURTESY THE FRESH CUT STIR FRY ALLIANCE

Ahoy there, Sylvia!

I recently went over to Holland to help with my grandson Eden's fifth birthday party. My daughter-in-law was particularly pleased to see me as she was not feeling well and there was so much to do.

I cleaned, gardened, made cakes, jellies and sandwiches, drew a treasure map (the theme was pirates) put up decorations and helped on the day to amuse and entertain 25 excited children of seven different nationalities.

It was exhausting but great fun and I was pleased to be involved. As we all collapsed in a heap after the last child had gone, my grandson looked at me and said: "Grandma, why did you come over?"

Sylvia Short (Grandma Sylvie), Arundel, West Sussex

Eden, Francis and Grandma Sylvia, all looking very scary!

My Prayer

Now my grandchildren have reached computer and texting age, this prayer means a lot to me, as I'm sure it will to other grandparents.

A Grandmother's Prayer
Let me give my grandchild gifts,
Not just toys, but other things
Like treasured dreams and memories
That gives a child both hopes and wings.
Let me help with little things,
To teach someone to tie a shoe
To answer funny questions too
And always know just what to do.
Let me show that what is old
A child may find completely new,
And know what once delighted me
Makes my dear grandchild happy too.
Mrs M Lomas, Cleckheaton

Plant of the week

If you want dramatic impact in a container, then you can't go wrong with a cordyline such as Cordyline australis. With its arching leaves and symmetrical habit a cordyline looks great planted singly, especially when you place one on either side of an entrance. Cordylines are not reliably hardy in this country so shelter them during the winter by bringing them close to a house wall. As well as plain green and purple-leaved varieties (shown), there are several varieties with Awards of Garden Merit including 'Albertii' which has green leaves with scarlet midribs and cream stripes.
● **Tip** – Remove well-rooted suckers from the base of the main plant during spring and transplant.

And another thing...

In 1930, Oscar Deutsch opened the world's first Odeon Cinema in Birmingham. ODEON stands for 'Oscar Deutsch Entertains Our Nation'.

Etiquette for Everybody
– 1920s' style –

On deportment...
Toes should be turned out, but not at right angles; knees must be neither too stiff nor too bent.'

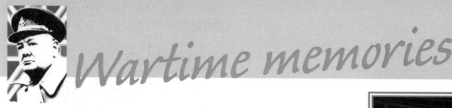

Wartime memories

Mrs Elizabeth Poland of Worthing has vivid memories of the night when German bombs devastated the centre of Canterbury

Elizabeth's grandfather (left) outside the Mac Fisheries store

At the end of May 1942, when I was four years old, my father was on leave from the RAF and I went with him and my mother to spend a few days with my grandparents. My grandfather was the manager of the Mac Fisheries in St George's Street in Canterbury.

We were woken in the early hours to be told the Germans were dropping flares and we all hurried down to the cellar. My grandmother was suffering from three cracked ribs after a recent fall and my 16-year-old uncle had had to have his leg amputated after a football accident at school. I myself had diarrhoea and, with no access to the toilet in the burning house, I was forced to make emergency use of a cardboard box instead!

My grandfather went upstairs to pull down the curtains in a vain attempt to stop the flames spreading and also to bring down my grandmother's jewellery box. Unfortunately, he brought the wrong box so everything was lost.

The bombing seemed to go on for ever until we were rescued by firemen who got us out over a wall. The scene I remember was of all the houses along the surrounding streets in flames.

My mother and I returned home to Worthing in a taxi, still wearing our nightclothes. When we arrived, we couldn't get in as mother had no key so a neighbour took us in and kindly boiled me an egg.

My grandparents were bombed out once again after this but I am glad to say that they survived the war – as did the clock in St George's Street that became well-known locally because it kept on going throughout all the raids.

Keen to be green *Everyday ways to save the planet*

- Dispose of your car thoughtfully. Your old banger may not be roadworthy any more but the spare parts are likely to be useful to someone. There is no need to break it up yourself as a breaker's yard will generally do this for a small fee.

- If your broken pieces of china are too pretty to use for drainage in garden pots, try advertising them in a local craft centre where they might be put to creative use in mosaics.

- Shoes that are too worn to give to a charity shop can be sent to the European Recycling Company, Whitehead House, 120 Beddington Lane, Croydon, Surrey CR9 4ND.

- Cardboard egg boxes and tubes from toilet rolls and kitchen towels are welcomed by playschools and nurseries where children use them for all sorts of creative projects.

- Aluminium foil that has been used in cooking can be washed, carefully dried and stored ready to be used again.

- To remove lavatory stains, make a paste of borax and lemon and leave for several hours before rinsing off.

In the garden

- Save old net curtains to fling over susceptible plants when a late frost has been forecast. Bubble wrap also provides handy insulation for delicate plants.

- Protect newly planted out seedlings and other young plants with cloches made from large plastic lemonade bottles that have been cut off at the shoulder.

- Cut plastic ice-cream containers into strips to use as labels when sowing seeds.

- Don't throw away the foil wrapper from your chocolate bar, cut it into strips and thread on to cotton to keep the birds away from your seedlings.

Quiz

Test your knowledge with this fun quiz. If you get stuck the answers are at the bottom of the page.

1 In what year was the Channel Tunnel linking England and France officially opened?

2 Who shot Lee Harvey Oswald on November 24, 1963 in Dallas?

3 What is the world's longest running stage production?

4 What is traditionally played on a bugle or drum to awaken soldiers in the morning?

5 What gas is represented by the symbol CO2?

6 In which now defunct soap opera would you have found the character Amy Turtle?

7 In Arthurian legend, who presented him with Excalibur?

8 Who famously said: "Any colour – so long as it's black"?

9 Who played Captain James T Kirk in the original Star Trek series?

10 The third Thursday in which month is traditionally Beaujolais Day?

11 Which comedian recorded the spoof single Funky Moped?

12 Robson Greene (pictured) formed a successful singing partnership with which other actor?

PIC: REX FEATURES

1 1994
2 Jack Ruby
3 The Mousetrap
4 Reveille
5 Carbon dioxide
6 Crossroads
7 The Lady of the Lake
8 Henry Ford
9 William Shatner
10 November
11 Jasper Carrot
12 Jerome Flynn

Who's a pretty

Joan Landymore is quite used to feeding the bluetits and sparrows in her garden, but then she had a quite unexpected visitor...

The most raucous noise permeated the quietness of a Sunday morning in my quiet village near Grimsby as I sat having breakfast. Tom, my neighbour, was already outside when I went to investigate. "What on earth is it?" I asked. "It's a parrot in the trees." Sure enough, there it was – very well camouflaged – perched on a holly bush. By the time I'd got my binoculars out for a closer look, it took off, flying past our gardens and into the trees beyond. That's the last I'll see of that, I thought.

The next morning I went down the garden and there it was, sitting on the apple tree with an apple in its claws. It was a beautiful green colour with pinky red flashes on its wings. I called and whistled to it, "Here pretty Polly," (as you would if you had an escaped parrot in your garden, I'll bet!) but there was no reply. Obviously not a talking parrot! And after dropping the apple, it flew off into the trees.

When it appeared again the next day I decided to contact The Jungle, a nature attraction at nearby Cleethorpes. They said it sounded like in African green Amazon and if they could find time would come and try and catch it.

In hindsight it was as well they never found the time. Great Coates is a small village and news soon got round that a parrot was loose in the area, and not long before I found out that someone had lost one. I felt like Miss Marple as I went round knocking on doors asking, "Excuse me, have you lost your parrot?"

In the meantime the bird was becoming quite a celebrity. The grandchildren couldn't believe I had a real live parrot in the garden and came to look and take photographs.

The phone rang, and a man introduced himself as Danny, who told me he'd lost a green parrot called Millie. He told me she'd slipped out of his garage when he'd let her out of the cage to have a fly round. He thought the best thing was to bring the cage to me and put it near where she perched and hope she might go in.

But Millie was very crafty. She was there the next day but not near the cage, just eating apples high up in the tree as usual. I had some monkey nuts in shells so I held one in my fingers to try and tempt her down. Although she didn't talk, I talked gently to her and suddenly to my amazement she started working her way down the tree. I held my breath and the next minute she'd carefully taken the nut from my hand with her beak, transferred it to her claw and broken it open. It was a work of art.

I was spellbound. She must have had about four peanuts, then just as quickly she worked her way back up the tree. I know I should have rung her owner straight away as he could have probably caught her but I just couldn't do it. She was so enjoying her freedom – and I was enjoying it too.

There she was in the tree

I felt like Miss Marple... "Excuse me, have you lost your parrot?"

girl, then?

again the next day, so my neighbours came round with a video camera to catch the action. We stood and waited, camera ready, and right on cue Millie came down for the nuts which I held out. The camera rolled, we couldn't believe it, she took the nuts gently from my hand then making a funny gurgling noise in her throat worked her way back up the tree beyond our reach.

I think she was feeling quite at home by this time, but more than likely she was getting tired of apples and nuts and wanted a change of diet.

Danny had left some birdseed so I decided to put some on top of the cage near the opening, thinking she might see it, come down, and go in. The next time I saw her she was calmly sitting on top eating the seed. "Sorry Millie, you know what I've got to do," I said guiltily and rang Danny to tell him she was on the cage.

He came round stroked her, then – one two three – as quick as lightning he had hold of her and into the cage. It was over!

It was sad but I know she had to be caught as he had told me she had a blocked nostril which needed treatment at the vets, and as the weather became colder, she wouldn't have survived. And she was lucky our resident sparrowhawk hadn't seen her or that would have been her lot.

Danny promises he'll see about building an aviary in the garden to give her a bit more space. I hope he does, I can't bear the thought of her having to spend years more in a small cage, although I know he does look after her well.

So, it was back to the housework which had been sadly neglected. There were still the usual blackbirds, bluetits and loads of sparrows in the garden but after an 'escapee parrot,' life seemed rather unexciting, that is until a small injured hedgehog appeared at my doorstep…

She was feeling quite at home by this time

Millie the parrot after her adventure

June 2006

Thursday

1

Friday

2

Saturday

3

Sunday

4

Monday

5

Tuesday

6

Wednesday

7

Thursday

8

Friday

9

Saturday

10

Sunday

11

Monday

12

Tuesday

13

Wednesday

14

Thursday

15

Friday

16

Saturday

17

Sunday

18

Fathers' Day

Monday

19

Tuesday

20

Wednesday

21

Summer solstice
Yours June 21 issue on sale

Thursday

22

Friday **23**	Tuesday **27**
Saturday **24**	Wednesday **28**
Sunday **25**	Thursday **29**
Monday **26** Wimbledon Championships start	Friday **30**

Flavour of the month

PIC: GARDEN PICTURE LIBRARY

'Another bride, another June, another sunny honeymoon,' goes the song and it is little wonder that this is such a popular month for tying the knot. What could be more romantic than a June wedding with the guests decked out in their summer finery and the departing bride throwing a bouquet of perfect red roses to her eagerly waiting bridesmaids?

Roses of every hue are now in their full glory. In our gardens, we can bury our noses in exquisitely perfumed shrub and hybrid tea varieties while along country lanes there 'blows an English unofficial rose'. There is even a rose called Father's Day which would surely be the ideal gift for horticultural dads on their special day, which falls on the third Sunday of the month.

All too soon, the longest day comes on the 21st, swiftly followed by Midsummer's Day on the twenty-fourth of June. Tradition has it that hazel twigs cut on Midsummer's Eve are supposed to be especially effective for water divining. But they won't be needed if another old belief comes true – that if it rains on St Vitus's day (June 15) it will continue to pour for the next 40 days.

If the weather has been kind, we should now be harvesting the first of the peas and beans we sowed back in March. And, towards the end of the month, the strawberries will be ripe enough to devour with cream while we watch the opening games of Wimbledon fortnight on television.

My Mum

He was very thin and shabby, and wheeled his rickety bike towards the children playing in the road and spoke to one of the girls. She called out to me: "Queenie, tell your mum that this man says he's hungry and wants some food." I went to the house and told my mother. We weren't any better off than other families in our road, but since my father had returned from France after the First World War he'd been in a regular job.

My mother came out and spoke to the stranger, then went back inside and made him a packet of sandwiches using the cold meat which my father was expecting for his evening meal. She also made him a bottle of tea, and I believe she also gave him a shilling. He thanked her profusely and then sat on the pavement leaning

Above:
Queenie's mother
Left: Queenie today

against the wall. Several of us stood and watched him eating but he was too hungry to be embarrassed.

I've no idea what my father was given to eat that evening – there were no freezers full of food during the Great Depression. I've always thought of my mother as kind, and this episode only reinforces that.

Queenie Hilder,
Peasedown St John, Bath

✚ YOUR GOOD HEALTH ✚

Mouthing off

Prone to cold sores? Sunshine can often trigger attacks, so protect your lips with a balm and avoid chocolate and nuts, as both contain the amino acid arginine, which can encourage the virus that causes the sores. Instead, include lots of foods rich in l-lysine, another amino acid thought to help suppress the virus – tuck into apples, pears, mangoes, beetroot and chicken.

My Prayer

The Driver's Prayer
Dear God, I pray with each new day
Be with me on the road,
And not allow me to get mad
With those who choose to goad.

Please help me stop my need to race them
At the traffic lights,
And calm my mind, so I don't make
Each journey one long fight

Whenever cars come shooting through
So they can be in front,
Remove desire to give their car
An ever-so-gentle shunt.

And when they drive too close behind
Or fail to indicate,
Let me not open up my window
And prevaricate.

For all of us, we like to think,
Our driving is the best,
But tensions rise in a hurried world
And our minds are filled with stress.

So when others lose their manners
And it's visible to see.
Dear God, I pray, with each new day
Let me start by changing me.

Mrs Patricia Longhurst, Romford

Etiquette for Everybody

– 1920s' style –

On farewells…

'When you leave her in the morning as you set out for business, kiss her and mean it.

TOP TIP

Remove stalks from button mushrooms and place a knob of cheese on each. Grill for 3 minutes and serve with garlic bread – delicious!
Mrs J Smith, Faringdon

Plant of the week

Whatever your skill as a gardener, you can't go wrong with hardy geraniums and one of the prettiest is G oxonianum which has clear pink flowers from June onwards. It makes vigorous groundcover and copes in most soils in sun or partial shade. H30cm (1ft).
● **Tip** – Plant it on a bank and let it scrambe with abandon – it will prevent soil erosion.

A treasured memento

Angela today

A postcard of some colourful lupins is one of my most treasured mementos.

In the 1970s our family went to a miniature train steam festival, where there was a stall selling pictures and postcards (mainly of engines).

"Which postcard would you like?" father asked our two-year-old, and he chose the one of lupins. "Why not a picture of an engine?" asked my puzzled father. "It's for my mommy."

Mrs Angela Harris, Wolverhampton

And another thing...
Ripon is Britain's oldest city. It was granted a charter by Alfred the Great in 886.

Passion Fruit Curd Tarts
(Makes 8)

● Grated rind and juice of 2 lemons
● 1 teaspoon cornflour
● 2 eggs
● 50 g (2 oz) unsalted butter, diced
● 175 g (6 oz) caster sugar
● 2 passion fruits
● 8 x 10 cm (4 in) ready-made sweet shortcrust pastry cases
● Icing sugar, for dusting

1 Place the lemon rind and juice, cornflour, eggs, butter and caster sugar in a small pan. Heat gently, stirring until the butter melts. Bring the mixture to the boil and cook for 1-2 minutes until smooth and thickened. Transfer to a bowl and leave to cool for 10-15 minutes.
2 Halve the passion fruits and stir the pulp and seeds into the curd.
3 Place the pastry cases on a baking sheet and pour in the filling. Leave to cool and set. Dust with icing sugar to serve.

RECIPE COURTESY TATE & LYLE

TOP TIP

I discovered that a melon baller with drainage holes is great for getting pickles out of difficult jars
Marjorie Cantwell, Dublin

My Prayer

As a young girl, I recited this poem during a children's church service, and have never forgotten it. It has been a great comfort to me over the years.

God's Telephone
Don't ever be anxious or worried,
You've nothing to do but call,
You forget you have telephone service,
To the very best helper of all.
Just calmly lift up your receiver,
And ask for the first on the throne,
Is Jesus there? So I am with you,
Speak Lord, for I feel tired and alone.
New trials have come to perplex me,
And what I should do I don't know,
So answer my prayer, Dear Lord,
And show me the way to go.

Mrs Thelma Hardman, Bristol

Etiquette for Everybody
– 1920s' style –

On manners…
'A woman with a baby and a number of parcels is an object for pity. Make her journey as easy as possible for her. You can give her a hand with the parcels.'

Plant of the week

Echinops ritro, commonly called the globe thistle, is a great architectural plant with spiky leaves and metallic blue flowers. It associates well with other structural plants especially eryngiums which are similar in colour, and silver artemsia. It thrives in full sun and partial shade and prefers well-drained soils. Divide large plants during the autumn. H60cm (2ft).
● **Tip** – cut the flowers and use them in dried flower arrangements.

A treasured memento

Betty today

My most treasured memento is my 1944 diary. I was 12 when I wrote it and it records my time in London and my country experiences.

Some things are hard to imagine now – sleeping under my bed, trying to sleep on the platform of Tooting Underground during air raids, watching a Doodlebug stop nearly overhead on Wandsworth Common and explode near to where my sister and I were standing.

As the bombing increased I was sent to stay with an auntie and uncle near Newbury, Berkshire. My diary describes what village life was like, how I went collecting crab apples, potato picking and gleaning in the corn fields in the autumn to help feed auntie's chickens.

And numerous entries of fun times, such as scrumping for apples with the local boys…
Mrs Betty Parkyn, Hythe

A RECIPE FOR YOU

Spicy Fish Parcels
(Serves 4)

- 4 white fish fillets, 175-225 g (6-8 oz) each
- 75 ml (3 fl oz) sherry vinegar
- 2 tablespoons dark muscovado sugar
- 1½ tablespoons oil
- 1 tablespoon grated ginger root
- 2 teaspoons soy sauce
- ¼ teaspoon salt
- ¼ teaspoon chilli paste or hot pepper sauce

1 Preheat the oven to 190°C, 375°F, Gas Mark 5
2 Cut four 30 cm (12 inch) squares of foil and brush each square lightly with some of the oil.
3 Place a fish fillet on each foil square.
4 Combine the remaining oil, sherry vinegar, sugar, grated ginger root, soy sauce and chilli paste or hot pepper sauce. Spoon the mixture evenly over each portion of fish.
5 Wrap loosely in foil, sealing the edges well.
6 Place the foil parcels on a baking sheet. Bake for 15-20 minutes or until the fish flakes easily with a fork.
7 Open the parcels carefully and serve hot.

RECIPE COURTESY BILLINGTON'S

And another thing...
'You know you're getting older when confronted by a most beautiful dress, you read the label and decide you'd rather get the guttering mended.'   *Pam Brown*

Looking after ourselves

I was about four years old and my brother, eight, and we were sent to Lewisham to queue for bread. The smell of fresh warm bread was too much for two very hungry children and we ate into the loaf on the walk home. Our angry mother gave us a wallop and made us eat the remainder of the bread dry for our tea.

Our mother left home and our father worked long hours, so by the time I was eight, my brother and I looked after ourselves.

Every morning I stood on the pavement, with a brush, comb and two elastic bands, waiting for a neighbour to stop running between her cleaning jobs, long enough to plait my hair and check my neck.
June Kimber, Sheerness, Kent

June (right) enjoying a walk

✚YOUR GOOD HEALTH✚

Best foot forward...
Dry, hard skin on your feet can break and get infected easily. Slough it away with a foot file, then treat your feet to a soak in a bowl of warm water with ten drops of antibacterial tea tree oil. Cut toenails straight across to avoid problems with ingrowing nails, and finish by massaging in a rich moisturising cream to help prevent the build-up of dead skin cells on your soles.

A RECIPE FOR YOU

Strawberry Cheesecake Icecream

(Serves 4)

- 450 g (approx 1 lb) strawberries
- 175 g (6 oz) caster sugar
- 3 tablespoons orange liqueur, eg Cointreau or Grand Marnier
- 250 g (9 oz) carton Mascarpone
- Biscuits, to serve

1 Hull and quarter the strawberries and place in a bowl with the sugar and liqueur. Set aside for 1-2 hours until the strawberries are very soft.
2 In a separate bowl, beat the mascarpone until smooth and softened. Roughly ripple in the strawberry mixture, then freeze for 3 hours or so until semi-frozen. Stir gently to break down the ice crystals. Return to the freezer until solid.
3 Transfer the ice cream to the fridge to soften up slightly, 30 minutes before serving.

RECIPE COURTESY TATE & LYLE

And another thing...

To take a dekko (to have a quick look at) was a phrase brought back from India by the British Army in the late 19th century. In Hindi dekho comes from the verb dekhna, meaning 'to look at'.

My Mum

Jean's very proud parents with their three-year-old daughter

Etiquette for Everybody
– 1920s' style –

On a gentleman's attire…
'It is not only what you wear that counts, but how you wear it. Do not put your hat on at a rakish angle; make your waistcoat seat neatly on your white collar; don't bulge your pockets out with odds and ends of papers; and see that no buttons are missing from your clothes.'

When I was just six years old at school in the playground one day, there was a crowd of children around a girl called Brenda. Obviously, I went over to investigate and was told she was adopted. I was very curious about this and went home to ask my Mum about Brenda.

She sat me down and told me that I, too, was adopted and that I was a very special little girl because I was chosen specially by them. The funny thing was that I didn't go to school the next day and tell anybody because I had a wonderful feeling and I wanted it to belong just to me.

Before she passed away, I gave Mum two lovely granddaughters, but she missed her grandson by just three weeks. How I miss that lovely lady. Anyone can have a baby but it takes love, devotion and a lot of patience to be a Mum.

Jean Boucker, Campeaux, France

TOP TIP

Keep a couple of spare sachets of white and brown sugar in the zip compartment of your handbag for emergencies.

✚ YOUR GOOD HEALTH ✚

Nod off...

If you have trouble staying asleep, your hormones could be to blame, believe it or not! The hormone melatonin, which controls sleep, decreases with age, and by 60 you produce half the amount you did at 20. So increase levels by upping your intake of the nutrients your body uses to make melatonin – these include vitamin B6, found in carrots, cheese, avocado, fish and spinach, and tryptophan, found in turkey, dates and bananas.

Plant of the week

Astrantia major, commonly called masterwort, is one of the best herbaceous perennials you can buy. It produces a haze of pastel-coloured flowers, all of which are surrounded by pretty green bracts and looks great in a cottage-garden scheme. There are many vibrantly-coloured varieties as well if you fancy something brighter. Astrantias thrive in sun or partial shade and will cope in most soils. Divide plants in early spring. H90cm (3ft).

● **Tip** – It self seeds freely, so transplant these young plants where you wish them to flower.

Drive on, Margaret!

To mark my 'three score years and ten' I decided to do something positive and started to take driving lessons.

It was hard work (but enjoyably so) and quite expensive, too. However, after 2½ years it was well worth it. Ian, my instructor, had the patience of a saint and was really wonderful.

Unfortunately, I had five failures with a manual car – gears and clutches were not my good points! I then had to have four months off for a (successful) hip replacement, and Ian then suggested I tried an automatic.

After ten lessons I

Margaret takes to the road

passed my test first time, much to everyone's delight! I'd managed to keep my lessons secret from family and friends, which was quite difficult at times, so it came as a surprise to everyone!

Margaret Godfrey,
Bideford, North Devon

My Prayer

Sanctuary
Are you always on the outside
On the outside looking in?
Are you searching for that something
Where do you begin?

Just close you eyes
And bow your head,
It doesn't cost a thing.
Talk to our Lord, and tell him
You need Him for your friend

Ask Him for forgiveness
Put your trust in Him
He never will forsake you
His love will draw you in.

Mrs Barbara Gibb, Stubbington

June 19-25

✚YOUR GOOD HEALTH✚

Herbal help for migraines

These debilitating headaches can leave you with nausea and sensitivity to light. If you're affected, try taking the herb butterbur – studies have found taking 50mg twice daily can cut the number of migraines you get by more than 60 per cent. Eating little and often, keeping your blood sugar steady, can also help.

TOP TIP

If you're going on holiday and don't know the lingo, learn to say 'please' and 'thank you' in the language of the country you're going to – you'll be admired because you tried!

A RECIPE FOR YOU

Lamb Kebabs with Orange and Watercress Couscous

(Serves 4)

- 675 g (approx 1½ lb) lamb neck fillet, trimmed
- 2 tablespoons harissa paste (see below)
- 1 tablespoon olive oil
- 225 g (8 oz) couscous
- Zest and juice of 1 orange
- 1 tbsp olive oil
- 1 each red, green and yellow pepper, cored and deseeded
- 1 x 85 g (approx 3 ½ oz) bag of watercress, roughly chopped
- 6 bamboo skewers
- To serve: watercress and wedges of orange

1 Thickly slice the lamb and place in bowl with the harissa paste and 1 teaspoon olive oil, tossing well. Cover and leave to marinate in the fridge for 2-3 hours. Soak 6 bamboo skewers in water for at least 30 minutes.
2 Place the couscous in a large bowl, add the orange zest and juice, oil and 450 ml (approx ¾ pt) boiling water. Season, then stir in the watercress. Cover the bowl with a plate and leave to soak for 15 minutes until the liquid has been absorbed. Fluff up the grains with a fork.
3 Cut the peppers into wedges and toss in the remaining oil. Thread the peppers and marinated lamb onto the soaked skewers. Cook the kebabs under a hot grill for 10-15 minutes, turning occasionally until chargrilled on the outside but still slightly pink on the inside. Serve the kebabs with the couscous, chopped watercress, and wedges of orange if liked.
- Harissa paste is a blend of red chillies, garlic, and spices such as caraway seeds and ground coriander and is available from most large supermarkets.

RECIPE COURTESY THE FRESH CUT STIR FRY ALLIANCE

Etiquette for Everybody
– 1920s' style –

On ladies' attire…

'While men should know a little about the current fashions, ladies must be a good deal more au courant. For them to be out of the running is to be nowhere. A judicious survey of the fashionable magazines is necessary, but a slavish following of the latest modes is not suggested.'

A coach trip to romance

It was 1969 and I'd just split with my long-standing boyfriend.

Fay on her wedding day

I was living in Dudley with my mother and went to spend the weekend with my sister in Worcester. She'd arranged for herself, her husband and I to go to London on a coach trip.

On the way there I noticed a young man on the coach with the most fantastic blue eyes and we kept exchanging glances. Coming home, he asked my sister if he could sit by me, and that was it! We met and married within three months and are still together after 35 years.

Fay Milner, Worcester

A treasured memento

Laura at her granddaughter's wedding

One day, when I was a little girl, my father came in from our vegetable garden and handed me a little, pale, yellow, semi-transparent, almost oval-shaped pebble. "Look, my dear," he said as he gave it to me, "you can almost see through it." So, I carefully put it away with my childish treasures.

Through the years I kept it, and when in my 20s, I had the idea of having it made into a pendant. I sent it to a London jeweller who set it for me in gold. The pebble hadn't needed polishing, for it had been naturally polished, having been in the earth for probably hundreds of years.

It has really been my lucky pebble, and still is. People have often asked me what semi-precious stone it is and are very surprised when I tell them my father dug it up in the garden in my Leicestershire village.

So the stone has great sentimental value to me, as in my mind's eye I can still remember the day my late, dear father gave it to me.

Mrs Laura Föst,
Llandeilo, Carmarthenshire

Plant of the week

Everyone loves sweet peas because they're pretty, have a lovely scent and, being hardy annuals, are simple to grow. The warm rosy-purple flowers of 'Sir Cliff' make it a great choice. The individual blooms are large and unruffled with a beautiful shape and distinctive light fragrance.

● **Tip** – Sow seed during autumn and overwinter the young plants in an unheated greenhouse and you'll have a great headstart in spring.

And another thing...

Melba toast is named after the Australian opera singer, Dame Nellie Melba (1861-1931)

My Mum

I'd like to share my wonderful Mum's 100th birthday in 2004. Lily had a great tea party with 40 members of her family around her: her three daughters (me, a Lily, too), Iris and Rose, eight grandchildren, 13 great-grandchildren and one great-great grandson.

The Mayor and Mayoress of Crawley popped in for a cup of tea, and to wish her well, and she received a lovely card from Her Majesty the Queen.

Left: Lily with her three daughters, from left: Iris, Rose and Lily
Right: Lily and her family celebrating her 100th birthday

+YOUR GOOD HEALTH+

What not to wear
In the warmer weather, your skin can easily be irritated by the wrong fabrics. Synthetic materials such as nylon and polyester encourage sweating, and may trigger conditions such as heat rash, hives, and thrush. Instead, choose clothes made from natural fibres like cotton and silk, which allow your skin to breathe.

TOP TIP

When going away on holiday, remove batteries from clocks and release watch winders to make them last a little longer
Mrs Beryl King, Poole

Etiquette for Everybody
– 1920s' style –

On wives...
'Where a servant cannot be afforded, a husband is not belittling himself if he helps with the housework. The romance of married life can be sustained even in the scullery while the wife washes the crockery and the husband wipes it.'

A birthday gift with a difference

Year Book readers might be interested to see this photograph of a trophy given to me for my 80th birthday. It was made by my niece's husband, Stephen, and depicts some of my hobbies over the years.

The body is a silver thimble and buttons, to represent my dressmaking. It's standing on a palette, and the arms and legs are paintbrushes, representing my attempts at watercolour painting.

The head is a cork and there's a string of plastic grapes (winemaking!) and the rose on the top is for my flower arranging and gardening. The tartan ribbon skirt was for my Scottish connection, as my late husband was from the Scottish Highlands.

I was thrilled to receive it, and it has been greatly admired by all my friends.
Doreen Wishart, London W4

Doreen, as her friends had never seen her before!

My Prayer

Mum Drina with Trudie on a walk in the woods

Plant of the week

One of the showiest of summer plants is the allium and 'Globemaster' is a welcome addition to any garden with its rounded heads of deep violet flowers. The flower-heads are enormous, measuring around 15cm (6in) across and the plants look great in mixed or herbaceous borders or in containers where they'll create impact on your terrace. Alliums thrive in well-drained soil in a sunny position. Divide overcrowded clumps during autumn. H 80cm.

● **Tip** – Leave the old flowerheads on the plants because they will create extra interest in the winter garden.

And another thing...

'The play was a great success but the audience a total failure.'
Oscar Wilde after the unsuccessful first night of Lady Windermere's Fan in 1892.

A RECIPE FOR YOU

Cardamom-scented Clementines

(Serves 4)

● 200 g (approx 7 oz) caster sugar
● 600 ml (1 pint) water
● 6 cardamom pods, cracked
● 6 tablespoons sherry
● 12 clementines

I composed this prayer about my lovely daughter, Trudie, who has been a tower of strength to us when life was difficult.

A Mother's Prayer
Every single night I say
Let me stay one more day
Let me see her matchless smile
Let me stay for a while

There is so much I don't want to miss
Her first romance, the meaningful kiss
It used to be her first party dress
Now it's the boys she wants to impress.

Let me be there to see the lace
The veil falling softly over her face
As she walks down the aisle with her dad
Please let us both be there for that.

I want to be there to see her first child
So we reach a new footing and smile
Two mothers together sharing the joy
Of maybe a girl, or maybe a boy.

I want to be there to see them grow
To see the pride in her eyes glow
I want to share all her life sends
To support and love her until mine ends
Drina Brokenbrow, High Wycombe

1 Place the sugar in a pan with 3-4 tablespoons of the water. Heat the sugar gently, stirring until melted. Bring to the boil and bubble rapidly, without stirring until the mixture is pale golden. Allow to cool for 5 minutes.

2 Add the remaining water to the caramel mixture, (take care because the mixture will splutter). Stir in the water until the mixture is well blended, then stir in the cardamom and sherry; return to the boil.

3 Peel the clementines and place in a large, heatproof bowl. Pour over the hot syrup and allow to cool. Chill overnight and serve. RECIPE COURTESY TATE & LYLE

Wartime memories

Ex Royal Navy seaman gunner Kenneth Smith witnessed the D-Day landings

I was aboard HMS Albatross, an ex sea-plane carrier converted to an emergency repair ship, and D-Day began on May 23 1944 when we sailed from Sheerness to link up with the main task force at Portsmouth.

Our voyage got off to an inauspicious start as the navigator managed to place our bows squarely onto the Goodwin Sands where we stuck hard and fast. We did not know which was worse, the indignity of this or the air attack we suffered from an ME 109. At the noon high tide, two tugs pulled us off and we were refloated.

We set sail for Sword Beach on the night of June 5. We were met by barrage upon barrage from the German gun emplacements. Our own fire-power added to the cacophony. The sight of our landing craft reaching the beach lifted our spirits – and the bravery of our troops as they scrambled ashore.

As the days passed there was plenty to be done. The hours of darkness were very trying; lookouts were posted all round the ship to counter German one-man submarines and E-boats.

On June 23, and again on June 26, the Albatross received direct hits. The damage was such that we had to return to Portsmouth for repairs. While we were there we received a few days leave before we returned – this time to Gold Beach – to continue servicing and repairing the landing craft.

During the morning watch of August 11, HMS Albatross was hit on the port side by a torpedo. Damage was considerable with the forward mess decks blocked by fallen lockers. Many of the crew were overcome by fumes from leaking gas cylinders and, worst of all, 69 were killed. Their bodies were retrieved when we entered dry dock at Portsmouth and all were buried at sea off the Nab-St Helens area.

♻ Keen to be green / Everyday ways to save the planet

- When giving your potting shed or workshop a spring clean, never pour unwanted chemicals down the drain. If you need advice on how to dispose of anything from bleach to weedkiller safely, contact the Environment Agency.

- When planning your summer holiday or taking day trips out to the country or seaside, think of leaving the car at home and travelling by train or bus whenever possible.

- Before clingfilm was invented, we simply put a plate over any leftovers or other food that needed to be stored in the fridge for a few days.

- Dressmakers accumulate stacks of offcut fabric that are highly desirable to patchwork enthusiasts. Take them along to your local craft shop or contact the Quilters' Guild. Website: www.quiltersguild.org.uk

- Save water by having a dual flush system installed on your toilet.

- Ice-cream containers are ideal for storing food in the freezer.

- Back from your summer holidays, you will probably have brought with you a good handful of foreign currency. A number of charities – Oxfam and the RNIB, to name but two – will be glad of this small change.

In the garden

- After buying bedding plants from a garden centre, don't throw away the polystyrene trays they are sold in – break them up and use them instead of heavy crocks for drainage at the bottom of a pot.

- Old car tyres have many garden uses; placed one above another they make compost bins or containers for growing potatoes. They can also be used to make swings for children to play on.

- Mulch flowerbeds to reduce the need for watering.

Have Vespa, will travel

Pat Williams shares some special Swinging Sixties memories, and introduces us to 'Miss Abigail'

In the 1960s, I lived in London and worked in a bank in Fulham's North End Road. The long street market outside was lined with cheerful Cockney stall holders who used to come in for change (pounds, shillings and pence of course) but also to spoil us with delicious bags of fresh fruit which they would pass straight over the counter. There were no bandit security screens in those days.

At the time, I was the proud owner of a little blue Vespa that I called Miss Abigail, and she drove me everywhere. One brilliantly hot weekend, I drove her down to Eastbourne to take part in a sea front parade with my scooter club. Miss Abigail looked very colourful, her aerial was decorated with flags. I slept on my own in a tent, in the middle of a very dark field but thought nothing of it. Very liberating and all that in the '60s. All that annoyed me were the raucous noises from other tents!

In 1963 I went to work at Head Office in Fleet Street, right in the heart of London and because I was 'Twiggy' thin in those days, I could wear mini-skirts and knee-high socks with my flatties. One of the perks of working at Head Office was the magnificent view every November of the Lord Mayor's Show, from the windows.

Another one was that I met my husband Gordon there and

Pat (and specs) during her time at the bank

we tried to conduct a secret romance, enjoying shared lunch hours in Lincoln's Inn Fields, at the back of the Law Courts, but in the company of other office workers! We had lots of after-work dates, browsing in dusty bookshops around the city and stopping off for a meal in one of the popular coffee bars – pub meals weren't really around in the '60s. In spite of being born in Liverpool, Gordon wasn't really a Beatles fan, but he did go to see them once at the Granada, in Woolwich. (And he's still got the ticket stub.)

Gordon and I married in 1966 and our son Ian was born the following year, in November. Ian was only 18 months old when I won a cruise to Norway. Ian took to travelling like a duck to water and insisted on staying up late one night so that he could join us for a dinner on the top of Mount Floyen. Our baby wasn't going to miss out on the swinging '60s.

July 2006

Saturday

1

Sunday

2

Monday

3

Tuesday

4

Hampton Court Flower Show (provisional)

Wednesday

5

Hampton Court Flower Show (provisional)

Thursday

6

Hampton Court Flower Show (provisional)

Friday

7

Hampton Court Flower Show (provisional)

Saturday

8

Hampton Court Flower Show (provisional)

Sunday

9

Final day of Wimbledon Championships
Hampton Court Flower Show (provisional)

Monday

10

Tuesday

11

Wednesday

12

Bank Holiday N Ireland (Battle of the Boyne)

Thursday

13

Friday

14

The BBC Proms begin

Saturday

15

Sunday

16

Monday

17

Tuesday

18

Wednesday

19

Yours July 19 issue on sale

Thursday

20

Friday

21

Saturday

22

Sunday

23

Monday

24

Tuesday

25

Wednesday

26

Thursday

27

Friday

28

Saturday

29

Sunday

30

Monday

31

Flavour of the month

Summer is at its height and July is the month to make the most of being out of doors. Food always tastes better when it is eaten in the open air and this is the ideal time for spur-of-the-moment picnics; pack up a simple repast of sandwiches and a flask of tea and head for your favourite beauty spot to relax and enjoy the view.

Alternatively, plan a barbecue in the garden for family and friends. No-fuss food is the key to success: tender new potatoes and a salad of freshly-picked crisp lettuce go perfectly with plainly grilled steaks or fish. To follow, the children will love ice-cream while the grown-ups dip into a generous bowl of the first cherries of the season. At Chertsey in Surrey a Black Cherry Fair is still held each year on the second Saturday in July.

Don't forget that both the very young and the elderly need to take particular care when they are out in the sun. Be sure to wear a wide-brimmed hat and apply a protective cream so that you can bask safely in the heat of the day. It is always wise to place your deck chairs in the leafy shade of a tree.

PIC: POWERSTOCK

In years gone by, the weeks from July 3 to August 11 were regarded as the hottest, unhealthiest time of the year. They were known as the 'dog days' because the period coincides with the rise of Sirius, the dog star – hence the name.

My Mum

Above: Kathleen and Ron's mother, Francis, in 1938
Right: Kathleen, author of the poem

'I'm enclosing a poem which was written by my sister, Kathleen, who is 83 years old,' *writes Ron Bignell.* 'Over the last few years, she has written many lovely poems relating to the family. A more wonderful sister I could not wish for.

'I believe the poem sums up all the wonderful things that a mother was and, I'm sure, still is for many people. The family situations described were applicable to many families but looking back, they were some of the happiest moments of our lives. Here is an extract:'

My Mother
Someone who was always there
With a loving smile and tender care,
Her presence and wisdom, beyond compare – my Mum…

…She was a friend as well as my Mum,
I worked with her to get household jobs done,
The washing and ironing, a mammoth job
She washed for others too for just a few bob…

…There was always a meal on the table there
When we came home from school, just plain fare,
No one could make a thing so good,
As my Mum's delicious Yorkshire pud…

…Search as I might, I would never discover
A being so wonderful as my Mother.

Kathleen McQueen

Etiquette for Everybody
– 1920s' style –

On personal cleanliness…
'A clean collar or a dainty blouse will not make up for a dirty neck, even though it be winter-time.'

A treasured memento

Above: Paul, aged 30.
Right: Paul's mother, Shirley

A school report belonging to my late son, Paul David Noble, is my treasured memento. Sadly my son, who was born in 1961, took his own life in 1992 – he was a beautiful, sensitive young man who couldn't cope with or resolve the problems he had. I was so proud of him, and when he died, part of me died too.

He filled the school report in himself on the last day of school before he left at 16 – the remarks showed he had a wonderful sense of humour. Here's an extract:

Geography, A+: *Paul is at the moment proving that the earth is indeed flat*
Art, A+: *Leonardo Da Vinci's Mona Lisa was yesterday removed from The Louvre in Paris – and need I say whose painting replaced it?*
Physical Education, A+: *Ran the marathon yesterday in less than four minutes*

Shirley Masterman, Worcester

Plant of the week

Agapanthus plants have an air of grandeur and are truly an aristocrat of the late summer garden where they'll add drama to your planting scheme. The exotic combination of graceful foliage and stunning flowers is equally impressive in a border or large container. Agapanthus requires full sun and a moist soil. The clumps increase in size rather slowly and should be divided during spring. H90cm (3ft).

- **Tip** – Agapanthus look best planted singly in containers because they're so statuesque.

My Prayer

A prayer of thanksgiving.
Thank you, Lord for my family and friends
For the love, the joy and sorrows we share together.
Thank you for revealing yourself
here on Earth in human form
To share my pain and suffering.

Thank you for revealing yourself through human hearts
In the form of love, sympathy and compassion.
Thank you for speaking to me through human lips
And comforting me through the touch of human hands.
Thank you for enfolding me in your everlasting arms
And catching me when I fall.

Thank you, Lord for just loving me.
Thank you, Lord of all

Malcolm F Andrews, Oulton Broad

TOP TIP

Pets can get suburned too. You may need to apply sunscreen to your pet's nose and ears

And another thing...

Carl Philipp Emanuel Bach, Beethoven, Jimi Hendrix, The Everly Brothers (both of them), Annie Lennox, Glen Campell are/were all left-handed.

A RECIPE FOR YOU

Creamy Smoked Salmon Noodles
(Serves 2)

- 30 ml (2 tablespoons) extra virgin olive oil
- 1 (350 g) pack fresh cut vegetable stir-fry
- 1 (300 g) pack fresh noodles
- 60 ml (4 tablespoons) crème fraiche
- 60 ml (4 tablespoons) hot water
- 175 g (6 oz) smoked salmon, thinly sliced
- 1 x 50 g (2 oz) bag wild rocket
- 30 ml (2 tablespoons) fresh snipped chives
- Freshly ground black pepper

1 Heat the wok over a high heat, add the oil and swirl it around, then add the vegetable stir-fry and noodles. Cook for 1-2 minutes, until the vegetables wilt.

2 Add 45 ml (3 tablespoons) of the crème fraiche and the hot water, and cook to evaporate most of the liquid, tossing occasionally. Add two thirds of the salmon, all the rocket and toss to warm through.

3 **To serve** – divide the mixture between two bowls, sprinkle over the remaining salmon. Place half the remaining crème fraiche on top of each. Scatter over the chives and black pepper and serve.

RECIPE COURTESY THE FRESH CUT STIR FRY ALLIANCE

TOP TIP

Water hanging baskets with ice cubes. They'll melt slowly and the water won't run out onto the floor.

A treasured memento

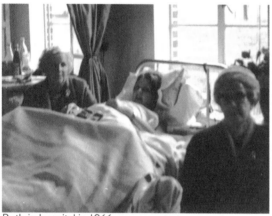

Ruth in hospital in 1966

In 1966 when I was 11 years old, I had to spend five months in hospital in Cardiff. During this time I had a hip operation and was in plaster for nine weeks, from my waist to my toes on my left leg, and to my knee on my right leg.

As you can see from the photograph, my left leg protruded out of the bed and unfortunately, people knocked into it, so my grandfather made me a little red flag to stick into the plaster to warn people to take care and avoid my leg! And the flag's my treasured memento.

During my stay in hospital, my grandparents were frequent visitors (my grandmother is on the right in the photograph). My grandfather used to travel three or four times a week to see me, although it involved three bus journeys. Sadly my grandmother passed away in 1977 but my grandfather, who was a true inspiration to me throughout my childhood and adulthood, reached the wonderful age of 91.

I will never forget either of them and my little red flag reminds me of all they did for me.

Ruth Tucker, Pontypool

Plant of the week

Actinidia kolomikta is a great climber with heart-shaped leaves which, when mature, have pink and cream variegated tips. It's vigorous and ideal for covering a large wall. Given the opportunity, it looks sensational if allowed to climb through a large tree. Although grown for its foliage it also produces scented flowers in early summer. These may be short lived but their perfume is lovely. Plant it in well-drained soil and in a sunny position and remove unwanted stems in winter. H5m (15ft) AGM.

● **Tip** – Plant a male and female plant close together if you want fruit.

Etiquette for Everybody
– 1920s' style –

On sitting…
'Just remember, whenever you are ill at ease, that most people are too preoccupied to think much about you, and that when you fancy they are scanning your face and clothes, they are really thinking about the next tennis-party or dance.'

Raspberry Sunrise

(Makes 2)

- 175 g (7 oz) fresh or frozen raspberries
- 4 scoops vanilla ice-cream
- 300 ml (approx ½ pint) chilled semi-skimmed milk
- I small pot (approx 150 g) raspberry yoghurt
- Mint leaves, to decorate
- Curly straws, for drinking

1 Reserve about four raspberries for decoration. Divide half the remaining raspberries between two tall glasses, crushing them slightly in the base of the glass with a fork.

2 Put one generous scoop of ice-cream into each glass.

3 Blend the remaining raspberries, ice-cream, milk and yogurt together in a blender or food processor. Pour into the glasses, then decorate with the reserved raspberries and mint leaves. Pop in the curly straws, then serve at once.

RECIPE COURTESY THE DAIRY COUNCIL

A seasoned traveller

Elsie taking time off between flights!

Who was it said, 'Life begins at 40'? Well, I've taken eight trips to Atlanta, Georgia in the past three years and am going again soon. While I'm there, I'm taking a free trip with my air miles to see near relatives in Miami and Los Angeles.

As long as my son-in-law is working in America, I'll try to continue. No, life doesn't begin at 40, mine started at 80!

Elsie Purcell,
Cheshunt, Herts

And another thing...

'Plunge a stone into a pond and the water moves in rings and ripples out to the bank; plunge a life in the ocean of the love of God, and countless other lives will be affected.'   *Unknown*

+YOUR GOOD HEALTH+

No more nausea

Travel sickness can ruin what should be a fun trip. Ginger can be a helpful remedy, so try taking capsules or just chew on a piece of fresh root ginger to help blast away nausea. If you don't like the taste, peppermint is another useful alternative – sip peppermint tea to settle your stomach before you set off.

A RECIPE FOR YOU

Spanish Omelette with Parsley and Olives
(Serves 4)

- 450 g (1 lb) potatoes
- 60 ml (4 tablespoon) olive oil
- 1 x 350 g (12 oz) pack fresh cut mushroom stir-fry
- 45 ml (3 tablespoons) roughly chopped herbs (flat parsley, rosemary, sage, thyme, oregano)
- 50 g (2 oz) pitted black and green olives,
- 8 medium eggs

1 Cook the potatoes in boiling salted water for 6 minutes or until just tender. Drain, then cut into 2.5 cm ($\frac{1}{2}$ inch) cubes.

2 Heat the oil in a large non-stick frying pan, add the potatoes and stir-fry for 5 minutes or until golden brown. Add the vegetables, herbs and olives, and stir-fry for 2 minutes.

3 Beat the eggs with salt and pepper, then add to the pan and count to 20. Stir the eggs with a wooden spoon, bringing the raw inner parts to the outside, and taking the cooked outside into the centre. Cook over a moderate high heat for 2 minutes, stirring three times.

4 Place the pan under a hot grill and cook for 2-3 minutes until golden brown on top. The tortilla is lovely eaten immediately, but can be left to cool and eaten the next day. Serve with salad leaves.

RECIPE COURTESY OF THE FRESH CUT STIR FRY ALLIANCE

TOP TIP

Pack items such as suntan lotion, moisturiser and perfume into individual bags, just in case the packaging gets smashed or the contents leak. Plastic or paper tissue folded around delicate clothes can help prevent creases.

Etiquette for Everybody
– 1920s' style –

On proper dress...
'We must not mix our outfits. A tailcoat and a cap or a flimsy blouse and brogue shoes reveal a disregard for details. This does not mean that an extensive and extravagant wardrobe is necessary. A little scheming can easily overcome such glaring combinations.'

And another thing...

Did you know a nightingale can warble up to 20 seconds without a breath?

My Prayer

Share His Love
*When we carry enough faith
In our hearts each day,
We'll feel God's saving power
His gentle guiding ways.
When we seek Him daily
In our thoughts and prayers,
We'll share His love with others
Upon life's thoroughfare.
By kindly thoughts and deeds
His will is being done,
For the Father loves us all
Each and every one.*
        Mrs Susan Bowman, Bude, Cornwall

✚YOUR GOOD HEALTH✚

Spot on!

Liver spots on the hands are common as we age. They're normally signs of cumulative sun damage, so don't forget your hands when you slap on the sunscreen. This should stop the brown pigmentation worsening. Liver spots can also signify a lack of B vitamins, so up your intake of foods rich in this nutrient – whole grains, eggs and poultry are all good sources. And try rubbing lemon juice, which has a gentle bleaching effect, over the marks.

Beryl and Margaret by the Spanish Bridge in Derry and Tom's roof garden

On holiday in London in 1946 my friend Margaret and I visited Derry and Tom's roof garden – the photograph is of Margaret and I by the Spanish Bridge. We took the lift to the 16th floor, and what an impressive sight the gardens were, and to be walking around one-and-a-half acres of beautiful garden, 100ft above Kensington High Street was wonderful.

There were many features – fountains, waterfalls, streams, stone archways, exotic flowers and shrubs – and a lovely view over London, as far as the Surrey Hills. I still have the brochure from that first visit, priced one shilling, and that is my treasured memento.

I visited several times more, during my honeymoon in 1949, again in 1951 and in early 1980, where to my disappointment it was sadly overgrown, although the Spanish Bridge was still there.

The gardens were first opened in 1938 and I often wonder if they have been restored to their former glory.

Beryl Lucas, Doncaster

Plant of the week

Acanthus mollis, commonly called bears breeches makes an imposing plant for your herbaceous borders with basal clumps of large handsome leaves. It may sulk a while until it's established but when it flowers, it looks amazing with stiff spires of purple and white hooded flowers. It cuts a striking figure in the garden, adding structure to planting schemes. Plant it in full sun or partial shade in well-drained soils. Divide large plants during the autumn. H1.5m (5ft).

● Tip - Water the plants well in dry periods.

My Mum

This photograph is of my wonderful Mum, aged 96. We had her down to stay with us in Swanage for a holiday and asked her if she'd like to go on a boat trip.

Ahoy there, Marjorie's mum!

Although she had a little difficulty getting on and off the boat (the captain actually lifted her ashore!) she loved the ride and really enjoyed the sun and sea breezes on her face. We bought her a captain's hat to mark the occasion and in the photograph she's wearing it with her sunny smile!

Marjorie Edwards, Swanage

July 24-30

TOP TIP

Now's the time to be looking round for the best winter deals – oil, coal, electric blankets, heaters etc.

✚YOUR GOOD HEALTH✚

Ban the bugs

Insect bites are a summer irritant. Stop bugs nibbling you in the first place with naturally repellant essential oils – add 10-20 drops of citronella, eucalyptus or lavender essential oil to an eggcup of sweet almond oil, then smooth the mixture onto exposed parts of your body. If you do get bitten, rubbing an ice cube over the area should take the sting out of it.

Skipping ropes and sweets

I can recall my childhood after the war; the man coming round with a handcart full of loaves; going to the cinema to see Uncle Remus. Not to mention the school Christmas parties, seeming to feature jelly, and bread and jam strongly on the agenda!

Not such bad times for this youngster, as I can still see the skipping rope stretched across the road with me hopping in and out, and still feel the handles of the scooter Dad had lovingly made for me out of the remains of the demolished air-raid shelter.

While grown ups with sad eyes – having experienced the heart of the Blitz – could always produce a sweet out of thin air for a good girl.

Gloria Dyer, Benfleet, Essex

A RECIPE FOR YOU

Mango and Passion Fruit Cheesecake with a Coconut Base
(serves 6-8)

For the base:
- 150 g (5 oz) desiccated coconut
- 175 g (6 oz) unrefined caster sugar
- 3 large egg whites

For the filling
- 250 g (9 oz) Quark (virtually fat free curd cheese)
- 400 g I lb) low-fat soft cheese
- 25 g (1 oz) light muscovado sugar
- Zest of I lime, finely grated

For the topping
- I mango, peeled and chopped
- 3 large passion fruit
- Juice of ¹/₂ lime

1 Preheat the oven to 180°C, 350°F, Gas Mark 4.
2 For the crust, mix together the coconut, sugar and egg whites in a saucepan and heat them over a gentle heat, stirring constantly until the mixture is warm (about 3-4 minutes).
3 Line a baking tray with non-stick baking parchment and divide the coconut mixture into 8 portions. Flatten each one out so that they are 7 cm (3 inches) each in diameter.
4 Bake them in the oven for about 20 minutes until golden brown. Leave the coconut bases to cool before removing them from the tray and adding the filling.
5 For the filling, mix all the ingredients together and spoon into the coconut bases.
6 For the topping, blend the mango in a food processor until smooth. Cut the passion fruit in half and spoon the seeds and juice into the mango purée. Add the lime juice and mix together well. Spoon the mixture on top of the cheese mixture. Eat straight away or refrigerate until required. They can be made a day ahead. RECIPE COURTESY THE DAIRY COUNCIL

Plant of the week

Alchemilla mollis is commonly called lady's mantle and is one plant every gardener should grow because it's so versatile. It thrives in sun or partial shade and makes great ground cover, quickly filling gaps between other plants in your borders. A charming little plant it has sprays of lime-green flowers in early summer and neatly pleated apple-green leaves. These look wonderful in the early morning when they catch dew drops and hold them like jewels. Divide large plants in spring. H60cm (2ft).
- ● **Tip** – Let it self-seed around the garden – it looks wonderful growing through cracks in paving.

Etiquette for Everybody
– 1920s' style –

At parties…
'Men must not stand in groups, smoking and talking. Such a habit leads them to become unpunctual.'

A treasured memento

My husband Bill and I knew each other from childhood. When the war started, Bill joined the Royal Marines. He was away abroad for three years, spending the last month in hospital in Sicily with malaria, jaundice and sand fly fever.

When he came home to London on disembarkation leave in February 1944 we became engaged. Bill went back to Scotland to join his unit but was taken ill again and was so bad his parents were sent for. Thankfully, he recovered and came home in July 1944. Knowing he'd be going abroad again, he suggested we got married during his two-week leave.

I don't know how we did it but we managed to book a church, I bought a white wedding dress, my sister was bridesmaid, and we had a wonderful reception at the church hall.

We were both very happy but the next day Bill wasn't well, and ill in hospital for two months. When he came out, he had three weeks' leave so we stayed with a relative on a farm in North Wales.

Mary and Bill celebrating their Diamond Wedding Anniversary

The first meal we had was chicken – a wonderful wartime treat. The lady of the house insisted I had the wishbone and I remember wishing that Bill would not be ill again. I still have that wishbone, as it means so much to me.

We celebrated our Diamond Anniversary in July 2004, so we have a great deal to be thankful for.
Mrs Mary Harris, Yeovil

And another thing...
'Age is not important, unless you're a cheese.'
Helen Hayes

Wartime memories

Gladys Newlyn of Woking recalls that even an air-raid alert could have its funny side

I was away in the ATS but my sister Joyce and brother Derek were still living at home when one night the air raid warning sounded quite suddenly. Dad was sitting in the scullery peeling shallots for his big pickle jars and he refused to go into our indoor shelter, preferring to take his chances outside.

So Joyce and Derek crawled in and sat there waiting for Nanny Lil to get in, but first of all the dog had to be coaxed to join them, then the budgie in his cage had to be handed in.

Nanny Lil's weight presented a problem and it was always better to let her manage on her own than try to shove her in from the rear. She got down on her hands and knees and was very gently pushing a lighted candle on a saucer along in front of her. She failed to notice our cat, Tiddles, slide in just ahead of her. His fluffy tail caught fire from the candle flame. Poor Tiddles! He squealed and flew out through the open back door.

Derek and Joyce were helpless with laughter. Dad, hearing the commotion, knocked over his shallots and gashed his thumb on his knife as he dodged Tiddles with his blazing tail.

Aghast, but quickly gathering her wits, Nanny Lil shouted at him: "Perce, put out that fire, the pilot will see the light!" Sucking the blood from his

Nanny Lil caused quite a stir

thumb and trying to retrieve his shallots, Dad did something he had never done before – he swore at Nanny Lil: "Don't be a silly beggar; there's no pilot – it's a doodlebug!"

Tiddles was last seen heading for the river at the bottom of the garden and he gave the air-raid shelter a wide berth ever after.

Keen to be green / Everyday ways to save the planet

- If you regularly enjoy a bottle of wine, save all the corks until you have enough to glue them together to make a handy noticeboard for kitchen or home office.

- The mercury in fluorescent light tubes can be recovered. For more information see website www.mercuryrecycling.co.uk

- Anyone who grew up in the era of rationing doesn't need to be reminded that, with a little imagination, leftovers can be tastily included in other meals. Boiled chicken bones make a nutritious stock and cubes of stale bread can be fried to make croutons for soup.

- Take unwanted old spectacles to Boots or an optician to be sent for use in Third World countries.

- If you're a silver surfer, don't forget that inkjet cartridges from computer printers are welcomed by charities such as SCOPE.

- Instead of pushing an unwieldy electric vacuum cleaner around, save electricity by returning to the older, simpler technology of the carpet sweeper.

- Share your car whenever possible; take a friend or neighbour with you on trips to the shops or supermarket.

In the garden

- Borage, comfrey or stinging nettle leaves can be used to make a liquid plant feed. Pack the chopped-up leaves into a plastic bucket or other non-metallic container, then weigh them down with a brick or stone and top with water. Cover and leave for around four weeks before straining off the liquid. To use, dilute to a strength of one part liquid to 40 parts water.

- Instead of using tap water in the garden, collect rainwater in a large water butt.

Quiz

Test your knowledge with this fun quiz. If you get stuck the answers are at the bottom of the page.

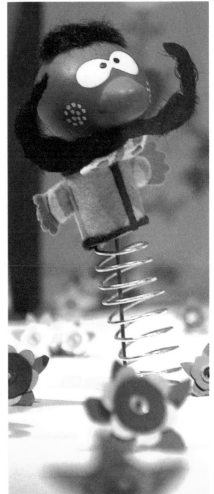

PIC: REX FEATURES

1 Which well-loved children's TV programme featured the character Zebedee?

2 Which Hollywood superstar was christened Marion Michael Morrison?

3 In which of Shakespeare's plays would you find the character Titania?

4 What is the French word for mushroom?

5 How many of Henry VIII's wives were beheaded on his orders?

6 Who was Britain's first Minister for Sport?

7 Who would use a quiver?

8 In musical terms, what does the term allegro mean?

9 What is the capital city of Ghana?

10 Which diminutive actor played Gunner Lofty Sugden in the TV comedy It Ain't Half Hot Mum?

11 How many British number one hits did Swedish supergroup Abba score?

12 Who is the foul-mouthed TV chef who also runs a restaurant at Claridge's in London?

1 The Magic Roundabout
2 John Wayne
3 A Midsummer Night's Dream
4 Champignon
5 Two
6 Denis Howell
7 An archer
8 To be performed in a brisk, lively manner
9 Accra
10 Don Estelle
11 Nine
12 Gordon Ramsay

Ground Force

by Rosemary Hoggard

Colin's garden has been his pride and joy but now he urgently needs some help...

From the conservatory, Colin watched the sturdy figure in a battered baseball cap starting up the petrol mower. He had never employed a gardener before. Since he became a widower, the garden had been his sole joy, but now the grass was straggly and weeds were taking over.

His new employee was tackling the neglect with enthusiasm. It seemed he had found a treasure when he saw the small ad, 'Active pensioner welcomes gardening work. Reasonable rates. No heavy digging.'

Colin hoped that when the heavy digging season came around, he would be back on his feet. Ruefully, he glanced down at his ankle; the plaster had been removed but it still wouldn't bear his weight without pain.

"You're an active pensioner, and I'm an inactive one," he'd quipped over the phone. The laugh at the other end was hearty: "We should make a good pair, then!"

Colin reached for his crutches – at least he could make the coffee. As he filled the kettle, the door opened and in walked his friend Hazel on a cloud of expensive perfume.

She gave him a peck on the cheek: "How are you today?"

"I feel better now I've found someone to do the garden. It's a load off my mind." He wished Hazel wouldn't march in without knocking but didn't let his irritation show. She'd been so kind since he'd stupidly fallen off his stepladder while clearing the gutters.

"You're just in time for coffee," he added, but

Hazel was staring through the window at the elderly figure emptying the grass box into the bin. "Surely a young lad would've been more appropriate?" she frowned, "OAPs are not good value."

"I'm an OAP myself," Colin chuckled, "that's why I get on so well with you."

"Hey, who are you calling old?" retaliated Hazel, but she relaxed.

Trouble had been averted, but Colin shook his head. It was the old story. For some reason, Hazel never cared for him being friendly with other people. There was the unemployed bus driver who usually sat on the seat in the park. He and Colin chatted about football. "The man's not your type," Hazel had decided. He sighed, and as he reached to open the cupboard, one of his crutches fell with a clatter.

"Let me do that," said Hazel. "Why do you need three mugs?"

"You and me, and one for Den."

"Den? So it's first name terms, already. How cosy."

Colin was not too sure how he and Hazel had become what they call an item. With her groomed blonde looks, he'd been surprised and flattered that she took an interest in him when they met at the Out-and-About Club. "It's time you enjoyed yourself, Dad," his daughter Jane had insisted, "and the Out-and-Abouts go on smashing coach trips." Since joining he had spent a great deal of time with Hazel – on coaches, and off.

She spooned coffee into the mugs, and said, "I assume the…er…gardener will be having coffee outside?"

"Well, I don't know." Colin was doubtful. "It looks a bit drizzly out there."

But the problem was solved when Den declined to come indoors, saying: "It'll take too long to get my wellies off."

The grass was straggly and weeds were taking over

Hazel relaxed. Settling herself in the window seat, she asked Colin for his shopping list as she was on her way to the supermarket. He felt a stab of guilt for his uncharitable thoughts.

The shopping list was dissected: "I think perhaps wholemeal bread instead of white. And some salad stuff," and "Colin! Not two packs of lager!"

Seeing Den trundling the mower down to the shed, Colin called through the window: "You've done a wonderful job! Same time next week?"

"We'll both look forward to it!" Hazel called out, keen to assert her relationship with Colin.

But Hazel wasn't always around when the gardener turned up and Colin got into the habit of taking coffee out on the patio where he and Den sat and discussed things close to their hearts – flowers, compost and fertilizer.

One morning, they were engrossed in watching damsel flies skim across the pond. Den broke the silence: "The pond needs desludging; that's my next project."

"I'll help – the ankle's not so painful now. I might have another go at clearing out the gutters."

"Remember you've got a metal plate in your leg," warned Den. "I know all about it from your daughter."

"Is there anything you don't know?" asked Colin with a grin.

Den gave a cough. "Er, just one thing…I

don't know why your lady friend hasn't been around lately."

"You're very mistaken if you think that!" Hazel stepped briskly out of the conservatory. Colin whipped round, startled. "And we'll be able to manage the garden ourselves in future; physiotherapy has worked wonders on that ankle."

"Hold on!" Things were moving too fast; Colin took a deep breath: "At the risk of sounding ungrateful, Hazel, you should allow me to make my own decisions. Den is my gardener, full stop. The job is permanent."

"Well, if that's the way you want it, you've seen the last of me! And you won't be welcome at the 'Out-and-Abouts' either!" She wheeled round on her stiletto heels and stalked off – or would have stalked if one heel hadn't caught in a crack in the paving, making her exit less than dignified.

Colin watched her go: "Talking of snapdragons," he said, turning to Den, "perhaps we can go to the garden centre one day to choose some for the far bed."

"It's a deal!" said Den. "But I agree with Hazel – you don't need a gardener any more."

"None of that, or I'll have to cultivate my limp again," said Colin with mock severity. "He leaned towards Den: "Incidentally, what is Den short for?"

"Denise – far too posh – everyone calls me Den."

Colin joked: "Well, Den, as you know so much, I'm sure you've guessed what's in my mind." He took her earth-stained hand in his. "Please don't give up on me – you suit me down to the ground!"

"Go on with you," she said, but she didn't remove her hand.

Colin looked at her sun-kissed cheeks under the peaked cap and thought she looked like a girl, not a pensioner. He decided to add love-in-a-mist to his list of bedding plants.

But Hazel wasn't always around when the gardener turned up

August 2006

Tuesday

1

Wednesday

2

Thursday

3

Friday

4

Saturday

5

Sunday

6

Monday

7   Bank Holiday (Scotland)

Tuesday

8

Wednesday

9

Thursday

10

Friday

11

Saturday

12

Sunday

13   Edinburgh International Festival begins

Monday

14

Tuesday

15

Wednesday

16   **Yours** August 16 issue on sale

Thursday

17

Friday

18

Saturday

19

Sunday

20

Monday

21

Tuesday

22

Wednesday	Monday
23	28
Thursday	Tuesday
24	29 Bank holiday (Except Scotland)
Friday	Wednesday
25	30
Saturday	Thursday
26	31
Sunday	
27	

Flavour of the month

In August we do like to be beside the seaside. Come the Bank Holiday and it seems as though every car in the country is bumper to bumper, heading for the coast. When we get there, we abandon ourselves to the time-honoured joys of beach cricket, sandcastles, whelk stalls and a stroll to the end of the pier while the shoreline rings with the excited shrieks of children splashing around in the waves.

For those who prefer to spend the break more quietly at home, there are plenty of tasks to be done in the garden. A pleasantly fragrant job is picking lavender flowers to dry ready for use in the linen cupboard or as a moth deterrent in your wardrobe.

Choose a warm, dry morning to gather rose petals that are just about to fall and spread them out in a warm place before using them with some of the lavender flowers to make a pot-pourri. Place both in a screw-topped jar with some dried scented geranium leaves and a generous pinch each of ground cloves, allspice and cinnamon and the fixative gum benzoin, then store for two weeks, giving the jar a shake from time to time. To enjoy the perfume, turn the mixture out into a pretty bowl and place on a sunny windowsill.

August marks the start of the harvest which begins on the first day of the month – Lammas Day – when it was traditional for a loaf of bread to be taken to church to be blessed by the priest.

My Mum

My Mother, Esther, was brought up in Shoreditch and was the second of eight children of Betsy and Solomon Shear. They were immigrants from Russia, fleeing pogroms and persecution rife in the late 1800s and early 1900s.

Esther was beautiful and she met my father, Hyman, when she was 17 and he 19. She became a fur liner finisher and was a fine needlewoman; she could also play the piano well.

They set up home in Leyton in 1929 and when war broke out and father went into the Army, we fled the Blitz, ending up sharing a house in Holmer Green, Buckinghamshire.

Mum cooked us lovely meals on the open fire in our living room, and also made cakes and biscuits when rations allowed. She worked in the evenings, sewing linings into fur coats for a furrier in High Wycombe, who would collect and deliver the work to her.

When my Dad died at the age of 69, Mum never married again, as they'd had a wonderfully happy marriage.

After she had a stroke in her 70s, Mum lived with us for 14 years, and when she died at the age of 93, she left a big gap in my life. She wasn't only my Mother, she was my friend, a very special person with a lovely nature and I miss her terribly.

Ruth Gold, Chigwell, Essex

Left: Esther as a young woman
Right: Ruth with Mum Esther
Below: Esther with daughters Ruth (left) and Maureen in the 1970s

A treasured memento

My memento is a receipt I still have from the midwife who attended the birth of my brother Andrew, in 1932, who was born at home in St Andrews, Scotland. The receipt reads:

Received – the sum of 15 shillings from Eileen Bloomfield in payment for one baby brother, with thanks, A Devine.

Mrs Eileen Smith, Hayes

Above: Eileen and Andrew on the beach in the 1930s

Plant of the week

If there's one annual you should sow this year, it's Cerinthe major 'Purpurascens'. Called honeywort, it's a beautiful plant which has become extremely fashionable in recent years. Bees love it and can be seen buzzing around the plants in summer. Simple to grow, it has fleshy blue-green leaves, mottled with white, and rich purple-blue, tubular flowers. It makes a great gap filler in your borders, growing happily in full sun or dappled shade but prefers chalky well-drained soils. H60cm (2ft).
- **Tip** – It should self-seed around the garden so keep an eye out for young plants, rather than buying more seeds next spring.

TOP TIP

Keep old lollipop sticks for using as plant labels.

Etiquette for Everybody
– 1920s' style –

On boys…
'Nobody objects to a boy who makes himself dirty; but everybody objects to the boy who stores up dirt on his person. Have a good wash – with soap and water – when you have finished some dirty job. Rub well round the eyes and nose and thoroughly do your ears. Do not forget your neck on a cold morning. Wash your wrists properly, and clean the black out of your fingernails.'

And another thing...

Uppingham School in Rutland has the largest playing fields of any school in England.

A RECIPE FOR YOU

Fusilli with Tomato, Basil, and Caramelised Garlic
(Serves 2)

- 175 g (6 oz) fusilli
- 45 ml (3 tablespoons) extra virgin olive oil
- 4 garlic cloves, peeled and sliced
- 1 large red onion, peeled and finely sliced
- 4 ripe tomatoes, roughly chopped
- 1 x 350 g (12 oz) pack fresh cut vegetable stir-fry
- 12 fresh basil leaves, torn
- 25 g (1 oz) freshly grated Parmesan

1 Cook the pasta in a large pan of salted water for 10 minutes or until just tender. Drain and set aside.
2 Place the olive oil in a wok with the garlic and cook over a low heat for 5 minutes, stirring occasionally until caramelised, then transfer to a plate. Increase the heat, add the onion and cook for 4 mins, stirring occasionally until golden.
3 Add the tomatoes and cook for 3 mins until softened. Add the vegetable stir-fry, garlic and cooked fusilli and stir fry for 2 minutes until the vegetables are wilted. Add the basil, half the Parmesan and season to taste.
4 To serve, divide the mixture between two bowls and sprinkle with the remaining Parmesan and a little more ground black pepper.

RECIPE COURTESY THE FRESH CUT STIR FRY ALLIANCE

And another thing...

'I want the whole of Europe to have one currency. It will make trading so much easier.'

Napoleon

My Prayer

I am never alone by day or by night
Or in any circumstance whatsoever
In the silence of the country
Or the hubbub of the town.
Whether I stand at the door of death
Or on the threshold of a new life
You are there around me
Bearing me up, guiding me on
Giving me strength.
You have been, you are ever
My friend

Mrs Dorothy Jessp, Ripley

Plant of the week

Cosmos atrosanguineus will delight chocoholics everywhere because its velvety, dahlia-like flowers smell exactly like chocolate. A Mexican perennial, it's popular in late summer as much for its scent as for its dusky brownish-red blooms. Plant the tuber at least 15cm (6in) deep – in sheltered gardens, it may survive with winter protection. If your garden is more exposed, lift the plant during the autumn. H90cm (3ft).

● **Tip** – Take cuttings during the summer to generate more plants.

A treasured memento

My treasured memento is a piece of stone. Thirty six years after the war my husband Tom and I took a journey down memory lane to a church in Italy where he was taken POW. It was a place called Pittsferato. The villagers opened the church for us and rang the bells, and a little boy gave me a stone for a memento to bring back to England. The church was up two mountains and you could see all the bullet holes round the church.

Mrs Muriel P Tutsell, Coventry

Left: An Italian friend putting a rock into Muriel's bag (but the one she brought home was a little smaller!)

Etiquette for Everybody
– 1920s' style –

On cheese...
'The idea still lingers that it is proper to eat cheese with a knife. The idea is wrong. Cheese is eaten by balancing small fragments on bread or biscuit, and held there by the aid of butter.'

A RECIPE FOR YOU

Summer Fruits Yoghurt Ice cream
(Serves 4-6)

- 500 g (18 oz) summer berries
- 150 g (5 oz) golden, unrefined caster sugar
- 600 g (1¼) lbs yoghurt

1 Trim and remove the stalks from the fruit and place it into a large saucepan with a tight fitting lid. Add the sugar and place the pan over a low heat for 5 minutes.
2 Purée the fruit in a liquidiser and pass it through a sieve. Leave it to cool completely.
3 Mix the fruit purée with the yoghurt. After checking for sweetness, add more sugar if prefered.
4 Pour the mixture into an ice-cream maker and let it run according to the manufacturer's instructions. Either eat it immediately, or pour it into a Tupperware container and freeze it in the freezer.
5 If you don't have an ice-cream maker, pour the mixture into a Tupperware container and leave it to freeze for 3-4 hours until slushy. Take it out of the freezer and put it into a liquidiser and blend it for a few seconds. Return it to the freezer for a further few hours until almost frozen. Blend it again. Do this a few times – the more you blend, the better the texture will be.

RECIPE COURTESY THE DAIRY COUNCIL

A caravan made for two

Joyce and Morris at their golden wedding in 2000

We met when I was 14 years old, and Morris was 15. He worked in a petrol station which I passed every day on my way to work as an apprentice hairdresser. We were engaged just before my 18th birthday, and soon after, Morris was called up for National Service.

We married in September 1950 and as we were short of cash, one of my hairdressing customers lent us a caravan at Holland-on-Sea for our honeymoon. It poured with rain all the week; our bed consisted of a converted settee with two mattresses which kept dividing into half, causing one of us to fall into the middle. We spent most of the night eating toast and laughing!

It must have been a love match, though, because we're still together after 55 years.

Joyce Stanley,
Hinxworth, Herts

TOP TIP
If you have trouble sleeping in hot weather, put your pillowcase (or pillow if you have room) in a plastic bag in the fridge half an hour before you go to bed. This will ensure you'll feel cool when you go to sleep
Pat Rolfe, Hornchurch

✚YOUR GOOD HEALTH✚

Soothe away sunburn
Had too much sun? Aloe vera can help calm redness and discomfort – just stroke it gently onto affected areas. Cooling natural yoghurt is another useful home remedy, and try tying a muslin bag of oats over the end of the tap as you run a bath to release the skin healing mineral silica they contain.

A RECIPE FOR YOU

Hot Barbecue Trout
(Serves 4)

- 2 green chillies, seeded and roughly chopped
- 4 garlic cloves, finely chopped
- 1 teaspoon black peppercorns, roughly crushed
- Large handful of coriander leaves
- 1 teaspoon salt
- 125 g (5oz) butter, melted
- 4 whole trout, gutted
- 2 limes cut into thin slices
- 1 tsp tandoori masala powder

For the salad

- 225 g (8 oz) small plum tomatoes, sliced
- 1 small red onion, finely sliced
- Handful of mint and coriander sprigs
- 1 tablespoon rice wine vinegar or white wine vinegar
- 1 teaspoon sugar

1 Blend the chillies, garlic, peppercorns, coriander and salt in a small blender for a few seconds. Add the butter and blend until well combined and finely chopped.

2 Place trout on a chopping board and slash the skin at intervals on both sides.

3 Cut 4 pieces of tin foil into large squares. Put the trout into the centre of each parcel and spoon over the spicy butter, smearing both sides of the skin and the cavity. Push a piece of lime into each slash along one side of the fish and sprinkle with a little of tandoori masala powder.

4 Wrap the parcels up, scrunching the edges together to create a secure parcel. Cook each parcel on a hot barbecue for about 8-10 minutes.

5 For the salad; combine the vinegar and sugar in a large bowl, then toss together the sliced tomatoes, onion, mint and coriander.

RECIPE COURTESY OF THE BRITISH TROUT ASSOCIATION

Etiquette for Everybody
– 1920s' style –

On shopping...

'It is well to remember that shop assistants have a very trying life. Customers should, therefore, save them as much trouble as possible. Ladies are the chief offenders; they will enter, say, a drapery store, will give the assistant the vaguest notions of their wants, and then show vexation when the correct goods are not offered them.'

My Prayer

A Prayer for the summer
Thank you God for such a lovely day
For all the birds that are singing
So bright and cheerfully.
For all the flowers that are in bloom
For the trees that give us shade from the heat of the sun
During these very hot days

June Johnstone, Camborne

✚YOUR GOOD HEALTH✚

Stand up straight

Your mother really did know best – bad posture is a leading cause of back pain. Improve yours by always trying to stand with your weight spread equally between your two feet. When you walk, hold your tum in and imagine that you have a thread attached to the top of your scalp, pulling you upright and straightening your spine. Pilates is excellent for improving your posture, so look out for a class near you or send an SAE to *The Body Control Pilates Association, 6 Langley Street, London WC2H 9JA*

Plant of the week

Artemisia 'Oriental Limelight' is one of the best foliage plants around with iridescent green and yellow leaves. Ideal in containers where it can be planted as a backdrop to summer flowers, it can also be grown in mixed or herbaceous borders as a barrier between plants which might otherwise clash. It dies back over winter, but will come back again in spring. H50cm (20in).

● **Tip** – Use it on its own in a brighly-glazed container to create impact.

In seventh heaven

When I left school at 15 in 1950, it was to start work in the Luton branch of Marks and Spencer, selling toys. Oh, I did enjoy myself, demonstrating how fast the toy cars would go, or how the doll at the end of the counter could close its eyes and go to sleep.

As a child I had never been given a doll, now I had a counter full of them, all to myself! I didn't want Christmas to come, as I was having such a good time.

Maureen Kerr, Bathgate, West Lothian

And another thing...

'If you're given the choice between money and sex appeal, take the money. As you get older, the money will become your sex appeal.'

Katharine Hepburn

My Mum

Marjorie's mother and father taken some time before 1914

This picture is of my Mother and Father, Mr and Mrs F C Hardy, who lived in West Ealing in Middlesex. It must have been taken a few years before the First World War. I have had the image enlarged from a very dark-metal negative of that period, but I hope readers will agree, it is a very pleasing picture of the dress of the period.

Regrettably, my mother died when I was five so I have but a few memories of her, but wanted to share my picture of them with you.

Marjorie Day, Seaford, East Sussex

✚ YOUR GOOD HEALTH ✚

Shut out the sugar

Did you know sugar weakens the immune system? It depletes the activity of white blood cells, which are responsible for gobbling up germs. Try these tips to wean yourself off the sweet stuff:

- Sprinkle sweet spices like cinnamon and nutmeg onto fruit, cereals and porridge instead of sugar.
- Swap fizzy drinks for sparkling water and freshly squeezed juices.
- Include plenty of sweet fruit and veg in your diet to satisfy your cravings – sweet potatoes, carrots, mangoes, bananas and dates are all good choices.

TOP TIP

Raise the cutting height of your lawn mower blades during the hot summer months to keep grass roots shaded and cooler, reducing weed growth, browning, and the need for watering.

A treasured memento

I have two treasured mementos – the first one is a religious birthday book given to me by my Sunday School teacher for good attendance at Sunday School. The year was 1931 and I was ten years old. It's called Forget Me Not and on each birthday remembrance is a passage from the Bible. The little book is held together with an elastic band.

The other treasured memento is a silk card, worked with poppies, leaves and golden mimosa sent by my late husband. 'To my dear fiancée', he writes, 'France-Belgium 1944. To my dearest Sweetheart, this card is just a symbol of my love and devotion and remembrance of you. Although we are miles apart my darling, this will bring me closer to you, in love and also in spirit. Keep your chin up in these dark and lonely days and very soon we will be together forever, never to part. Cheerio, my darling Sweetheart. All my love and thoughts are for you.

Your ever loving and devoted Sweetheart, John.'

Mrs Patricia Jackson, Chichester

A RECIPE FOR YOU

Italian White Trifle with Summer Berries
(Serves 6 – 8)

- 4 tablespoons white rum
- 8 sponge fingers
- 2 x 250 g (9 oz) cartons of mascarpone
- 400 g (1 lb) carton fresh custard
- 6 meringue nests
- 450 ml (approx ¾ pint) double cream
- Few drops vanilla extract
- 2 tablespoons icing sugar
- 300 g (approx 11 oz) fresh berries such as raspberries

1 Dip the sponge fingers into the rum and layer into a glass serving bowl.
2 Place the mascarpone in a large bowl and beat until smooth. Gradually beat in the custard, then crumble in the meringues. Spoon over the sponge fingers and place in the fridge.
3 Lightly whip the cream until it forms soft peaks, then whisk in the vanilla extract and icing sugar. Roughly spoon the cream on top of the custard, then decorate with the fruit. Chill until ready to serve.

RECIPE COURTESY TATE & LYLE

Wartime memories in Granny's pub

Mousehole in the skirting board
Sawdust spittoons on the floor
Blackout curtains neatly arranged
Over criss-cross tape on window panes.

Washday Monday – just cold meat
Eating dinner in the heat
Steaming copper, bleached white stick
Blowflies dodging the sticky strip.

Liberty bodice and 'sensible' shoes
Out with the sack for rabbit food
Soft shrivelled apples wrapped airtight
Syrup of Figs on Friday, bath night.

Parting of hair, inspection of head
Grandad's truss hanging
in the shed
Dried milk, dried egg and
cod liver oil
Smell of meths from the Gents' urinal.

Sunday sermons – then a bore
Afternoon in silence watching Gran snore
Must keep quiet and never stir
Mum's henna'd head in newspaper.

Painted legs to imitate hose
Throbbing chilblains on my toes
On their heads, the girls wore snoods
And in the papers, depressing news.

Joy Reeve, St Neots, Cambs

Plant of the week

Gazania 'Red Stripe' has large golden orange flowers, each with a maroon stripe and is an excellent choice to enliven your sunny borders and patio containers. It's best grown as a half hardy annual and will flower throughout the summer. If you haven't sown seed during spring, you can buy plants from garden centres during the summer. H25cm (10in).

● **Tip** – you can overwinter plants in a frost-free greenhouse because they're perennial just tender.

And another thing...

The phrase, 'Put a sock in it' comes from the days of the early gramophones which had large horns through which the sound was amplified. They had no volume control, so a sock was used to turn the sound down.

Etiquette for Everybody
– 1920s' style –

On smoking...
'In smoking carriages of trains, your smoke should be so negotiated that it does not encircle your neighbour who is not smoking. The fact that the carriage is labelled 'Smoking' does not entitle you to neglect this matter.'

Wartime memories

Mrs Joyce Masters of Hayle in Cornwall says being in the Land Army proved to be the happiest time of her life

Joyce - second from left

During the Blitz, I lived with my family in London and worked at the Treasury in Whitehall. Travelling to work, I saw fresh damage every day, whole roads flattened and people digging in the rubble.

One night, we were in the Andersen shelter and my mother was counting the thuds as the bombs hit the ground. She was very scared until my brother said: "Listen!" and it turned out to be my father who had fallen asleep and was snoring! For the first time in weeks, we all started laughing.

When I reached the age of 18, I joined the Women's Land Army. In 1941 I went to Cornwall where I was billeted in a hostel with other girls and worked on Trewinnard Farm at St Erth. It was a different world.

It was hard work, cutting cabbage and broccoli, but very rewarding. Digging sugar beet and potatoes were both muddy jobs. I looked forward to haymaking and the harvest. The farmer's wife used to cook pasties and cakes and bring them out to the fields at 'crib' time. The rest of the year we had packed lunches from the hostel, made the day before and dried up at the edges.

We were cutting cabbages one morning, ready to be put on the 12 o'clock train, when the housekeeper came to the field gate and shouted at us: "It has just now been announced on the wireless – the war is over!"

Needless to say, the cabbages we were cutting were thrown in the air. We danced and sang and had a cabbage fight. The cabbages were never put on the railway truck.

The story has a happy ending as I settled in Cornwall after marrying my boyfriend who was the horseman on the farm.

Keen to be green Everyday ways to save the planet

- When insulating your loft, use natural materials such as cellulose fibre or vermiculite instead of polyurethane foam or polystyrene products.

- Never leave the fridge door open longer than necessary as this allows cold air to escape.

- For cleaning windows, use a solution of one part white vinegar to one part water.

- When buying a new car, remember that diesel contains more pollutants than petrol. If you wish to use diesel for reasons of economy, low-sulphur diesel is more environmentally friendly.

- Put a stop to wasteful junk mail by writing to the Mailing Preference Service, *FREEPOST 29 LON 20771, London W1E 0ZT*

- When buying kitchen towel and toilet rolls, always choose ones made from recycled paper.

- Don't take it with you when you're gone! If you would prefer not to be buried or cremated in a wooden coffin, include clear instructions to this effect in your will. Alternatives include a woollen shroud or cardboard coffin. Visit the website www.greenburials.co.uk for more information.

- Be wary of using disposable cameras as less than 50 per cent of these are recycled (despite the claims made on the box). If you do use one, ensure that the developer you take it to will recycle the remains.

In the garden

- Put all uncooked vegetable waste from the kitchen on to the compost heap. Torn up paper can also be added in small quantities.

- Used sink and bath water is fine for watering the garden.

Brian setting off on a flight in his second home-built plane

High flying into retirement

After years of working in a shop, Jutta Marshall approached retirement with trepidation. But eight years on, she and husband Brian have fulfilled more dreams than they ever thought possible...

Having worked in the family business for 45 years my husband Brian couldn't wait for the end of 1998. An energetic 65-year-old, he had big plans for his retirement! There'd be more time for his favourite sport, golf, and the chance to gain his pilot licence for the light aircraft he'd built from a kit in our garage.

But I didn't share my husband's enthusiasm for our coming retirement. Lacking

Jutta in 2000, signing her autobiography

Brian's sporting and technical ability, I wondered if there were enough activities to fill our newly found leisure time.

My thoughts took me back to a time before I was part of Marshall's Jewellers. A native of Austria, I'd been a teacher for eight years before meeting Brian on a study trip to London. We married in 1964 and I happily become a full-time housewife and mother in England.

With the boys at school I worked part-time as a German tutor and occasionally helped out in our business. I had enjoyed working with Brian but now our working life had come to the end of the road.

My attempts to take up golf as a hobby failed so I pursued the arts. And learning new techniques with modern mediums at an art club, I re-discovered my passion for painting.

My greatest triumph, however,

came in 2000 when my autobiography was published. Entitled The White Rose and the Swastika, it spans 25 years of my life, from my childhood under Hitler to my marriage and move to Yorkshire.

My writing these days concentrates on stories and articles for newspapers and magazines. I enjoy meeting like-minded people at two art clubs and having conquered my initial fear of flying, am now an enthusiastic passenger in Brian's second home-built microlite plane.

However, the highlight of our retirement, so far, was the marriage of our son, Robert, to a French girl in 2001 and the arrival of our first grandchild, Jonathan. What a good excuse to visit France and even Oklahoma where our young family live at the moment.

Who says retirement can't be the most fulfilling and exciting time of your life? Not us!

September 2006

Friday

1

Saturday

2

Sunday

3

Monday

4

Tuesday

5

Wednesday

6

Thursday

7
                                        Burghley Horse Trials

Friday

8
                                        Burghley Horse Trials

Saturday

9
                                        Burghley Horse Trials
                                        Last night of the BBC Proms

Sunday

10
                                        Burghley Horse Trials

Monday

11

Tuesday

12

Wednesday

13
Yours September 13 issue on sale

Thursday

14

Friday

15

Saturday

16

Sunday

17

Monday

18

Tuesday

19

Wednesday

20

Thursday

21

Friday

22

Saturday	Wednesday
23	27
Sunday	Thursday
24	28
Monday	Friday
25	29
Tuesday	Saturday
26	30

Flavour of the month

Opinion is divided as to whether September is the last month of summer or the first one of autumn but everyone agrees that it is the mellowest month of all. The sun shines less fiercely and there is a fresher feel to September days.

This is a busy time for cooks wishing to make the most of a bountiful supply of fruit and vegetables before the season is over. The kitchen is a hive of activity with surplus tomatoes, apples, onions and other produce being prepared for the freezer or turned into jams and chutneys for the store cupboard.

The whole family can join in a blackberrying expedition, equipped with walking sticks to pull down hard-to-reach boughs and baskets to carry home enough fruit to make a delicious blackberry and apple crumble that can be eaten right away, as well as blackberry jelly to be enjoyed with scones on a winter's afternoon.

Anyone who walks out on a September morning won't fail to see hundreds of spiders' webs draped on bushes and fences, glistening with dewdrops. Spiders are especially evident at this time of the year and, to the horror of those who fear them, often come indoors for warmth. But before you kill the eight-legged hairy monster that has scuttled out from under the settee, consider the old saying, 'If you wish to live and thrive, let the spider run alive.'

Heaths and moorland are purple with heather while in our gardens Michaelmas daisies are coming into bloom. Their name comes from the feast of St Michael which falls on September 29.

PIC: FOTEX MEDIEN AGENTUR GMBH/REX FEATURES

My Mum

I'm 70 years old and can still remember how wonderful my Mum, Mary, was. With my Dad, who was the village policeman, she raised five of us children in a two-up, two-down terraced house.

The sitting room was kept clean and tidy for visitors. She did all her own baking, washing and ironing, and the toilet was outside across the yard. We were a happy family brought up in a loving Christian home.

At the age of 95, she went to live in a nursing home in Durham City where she was very happy. I telephoned her every Sunday and my husband would take me from Harrogate to visit her. He would go to town and I would spend precious time with her doing her nails and hair, tidying cupboards and drawers – whatever she wanted. We always had a good laugh and a lot of cuddles.

In 2002 she passed peacefully away, aged 100 years after a wonderful life. I still miss her very much but I'm so thankful for having her for so long.

Ann Harriman,
Harrogate

Above: Mary (aged 95) with daughter Ann (a mere 61!)
Left: Mary's 100th birthday with sons, from left: Frank, Peter and John. Front row Ann (left) and sister Betty with Mary

Etiquette for Everybody
– 1920s' style –

On letter writing…
'Do not type letters to friends. Never write in pencil unless it is a very hurried note to a very intimate acquaintance. And never use red ink at all.'

TOP TIP

For scooping compost out of a bag, take a one litre empty milk carton and cut it into a scoop with the handle on for scooping. Very handy!
Mrs J Johnstone,
Camborne

✚YOUR GOOD HEALTH✚

Getting mouthy

Good oral hygiene is particularly vital as you get older. Gums can begin to erode with age, so look after them by flossing every day. Use a plastic tongue scraper (from chemists) to gently remove bacteria, and spend three minutes brushing your teeth – that's about the length of your favourite song! Finish up with a mouth wash. If you have inflamed gums or a mouth ulcer, try rubbing a little clove essential oil on the area for instant relief. And don't forget to keep that dentist's appointment…

A treasured memento

My memento is my grandmother's brass, long handled toasting fork. My husband and I had an open fire and Parkray for 34 years of our married life. Toast always tasted better made on the fire. Toast with dripping, toast with butter – what could be better on a cold, winter's day? My grandma cleaned the brass every week, and it was glowing on Sunday afternoon, when we paid our weekly visit.
Mrs Diana Royal, Stowmarket

Eileen's toasting fork

Plant of the week

Crocosmias originate in South Africa and will add scorching highlights to your borders with their fiery yellow, orange or red flowers. There are numerous varieties to choose between, all of which are simple to grow. Choose a sunny position and well-drained soil and leave them to it! Divide congested clumps during the spring. H65cm (26in).
- **Tip** – plant them among airy grasses to create a magical effect in late summer.

My Prayer

Dear God, are you busy today?
Have you time to hear what I say?
I know there are thousands of others
Loved ones, fathers and mothers
That you alone can bring relief
Dear God, are you busy today?

Dear God, are you busy today?
Have you time to hear what I say
Am I one lost voice in a crowd?
Will it help if I shout out loud?

Please listen while I pray
For a loved one far away

Please God
Dear God
Don't be busy today
Margaret Norgan, Harlow

A RECIPE FOR YOU

Herby Lemon Vegetables with Watercress
(Serves 2)

- 30 ml (2 tablespoons) extra virgin olive oil
- 45 ml (3 tablespoons) fresh chopped mixed herbs (rosemary, thyme, oregano, sage or tarragon)
- Zest and juice ½ lemon
- 1 x 350 g (12 oz) pack fresh cut vegetable stir fry
- 1 x 85 g (approx 3½ oz) pack watercress
- 30 ml (2 tablespoons) dark soy sauce
- Freshly ground black pepper

1 Heat the wok up on a high heat, then add the olive oil and swirl it around. Add the fresh herbs, then stir them to release their aroma, then add the lemon and vegetables.
2 Cook for 2 minutes, stirring until the vegetables are just wilted. Add a few tablespoons of hot water, the watercress and soy sauce and cook another minute.
3 Season with plenty of ground black pepper and serve. This makes a lovely side dish to serve with fish or chicken, with the watercress giving a really peppery flavour to the vegetables. RECIPE COURTESY THE FRESH CUT STIR FRY ALLIANCE

And another thing...

'When I think of God, my heart is so filled with joy that the notes fly off as from a spindle.'
Joseph Haydn (1732-1809)

And another thing...

One night, a father overheard his son pray, 'Dear God, make me the kind of man my daddy is.' Later that night, the father prayed, 'Dear God, make me the kind of man my son wants me to be.'

Anon

My Prayer

I love reading verses to the elderly friends I visit; one lady told me some that I hadn't come across before, including this one.

Give me a sense of humour, Lord
The grace to see a joke
To get some happiness from life
And pass it on to folk

Marjorie Hotston-Moore, Dorset

Plant of the week

Eucomis bicolor, the pineapple lily, is always a talking point, with flowers that, as its common name suggests, resemble a pineapple. It produces spectacular spikes of purple-edged, pale green flowers in August, topped with a pineapple-like tuft. It's a great choice for a large, well-drained container in a sunny, exotic-style garden. H90cm (3ft).

● **Tip** – It's not fully hardy in frost-prone areas so over-winter it in a cool greenhouse.

A treasured memento

Emily with Mount Ranier in the background

In September 1980 I had a memorable six-week holiday in Canada. I spent two weeks with a friend who lived in Winnipeg, then four weeks with another friend in British Columbia, who arranged a long weekend in Seattle Washington State.

We travelled by coach and as we neared Seattle the sky darkened, the coach driver calmly assuring us that it was probably Mount St Helens erupting again.

A couple of days later, as we travelled to see Mount Ranier, we could see the ash from Mount St Helens settling thick everywhere.

One lad on the coach had a large bag and was collecting the ash for his dad – apparently it was excellent fertiliser. I only had a small paper bag but the ash I brought back now sits in pride of place in a small jar in a corner cupboard with other treasures – a memento of a wonderful holiday!

Mrs Emily Soper, Gosport

TOP TIP

Soak two or three cotton wool pads with some lavender water and put in your undies drawer – makes your lingerie smell lovely!

A RECIPE FOR YOU

Baked Apples With Butterscotch Sauce

- 110 g (4 oz) butter
- 110 g (4 oz) light muscovado sugar
- 110 g (4 oz) dried cranberries
- 110 g (4 oz) walnuts
- 4 tablespoons cider or apple juice
- 1 teaspoon ground cinnamon (optional)
- 4 large Bramley apples

For the butterscotch sauce
- 110 g (approx 4 oz) unsalted butter
- 110 g (approx 4 oz) light muscovado sugar
- 150 ml (1/4 pint) double cream
- Half a teaspoon vanilla extract

1 Preheat the oven to 200°C, 400°F Gas Mark 6.
2 Cream 2/3 of the butter with the sugar until soft, then stir in the cranberries and walnuts.
3 Peel and core the apples and place them in a greased ovenproof baking dish. Score round the middle of each apple with a sharp knife.
4 Spoon the mixture into the centre of each apple. Dot with the remaining butter and sprinkle with the cinnamon if using. Pour the cider or apple juice over and around the apples.
5 Cook for 15-20 minutes or until soft.
6 For the sauce: Put all the ingredients into a pan over a low heat and stir until the butter has melted and the sugar has dissolved.
7 Boil the sauce for about 3-4 minutes, and as it boils the sauce will thicken.
8 Remove the apples from the oven and serve with the sauce.
- This recipe contains nuts   RECIPE COURTESY BILLINGTON'S

Butlins by the sea

Left: Kay getting out of the pool
Right: Kay and her mum at Butlins

In the 1950s my mum and dad always went to Butlins holiday camp at Clacton-on-Sea for a week's holiday.

I was 12 years old when the photograph of me was taken at the outdoor swimming pool, wearing my new red and white swimming costume. The indoor pool behind me was great and had a continental look inside.

The other photograph is of my mum and me outside the dance hall. Butlins has sadly now become a housing estate, but I still have happy memories of good family holidays there.

Kay Probert, Shoeburyness, Essex

Etiquette for Everybody
– 1920s' style –

On men sitting…
'On sitting down, do not cross the legs. It is wonderfully comforting to do so, but save that up until you retire to the smoking den.'

✚YOUR GOOD HEALTH✚

Feeling touchy
Hugs and cuddles don't just help us feel good – research has shown they can help lower blood pressure, too. Get your partner to gently massage some body lotion or even plain olive oil into your back and shoulders to help those stresses and strains melt away. Studies have found stroking pets has a similar effect, so give Rover or Whiskers plenty of pampering!

A RECIPE FOR YOU

Hot Seared Beef Salad With New Potatoes and Honey Dressing

(Serves 4)

- 450 g (approx 1 lb) lean beef rump or sirloin steak
- 375 g (approx 12 oz) new potatoes
- 1 medium cucumber
- Flat leaf parsley, chopped
- 40 g (1½ oz) flaked almonds or pine nuts, toasted
- 75 ml (5 tablespoons) extra virgin olive oil
- 30 ml (2 tablespoons) sherry vinegar
- 30 ml (2 tablespoons) runny honey
- 100 g (4 oz) mixed salad leaves
- 8 cherry tomatoes

1 Peel and halve the new potatoes and cook in boiling salted water for 10-15 minutes, or until tender. Drain and set aside.

2 Slice the cucumber into a large bowl with the flat leaf parsley and flaked almonds or pine nuts. Add the warm potatoes.

3 For the dressing, whisk together 60 ml (4 tablespoons) extra virgin olive oil, the sherry vinegar and runny honey in a bowl, and season.

4 Heat 15 ml (1 tablespoon) extra virgin olive oil in a pan and fry the lean beef steaks according to preference. Season and set aside to rest for 5-10 minutes.

5 Cut the beef into 5 cm (2 inch) strips and add to the remaining salad ingredients. Pour any beef juices from the pan into the salad dressing.

6 Arrange the mixed salad leaves on a large plate, scatter 8 halved cherry tomatoes over, and spoon over half the dressing.

7 Pile the beef and potato salad over the salad leaves. Add the remaining dressing and garnish with extra sprigs of flat leaf parsley.

RECIPE COURTESY THE ENGLISH BEEF AND LAMB EXECUTIVE

Etiquette for Everybody
– 1920s' style –

On personal cleanliness…
'…do not dislodge foreign matter from the nails with your railway ticket whilst sitting on the Tube.'

TOP TIP

Always keep a pair of comfy shoes in a place where you spend a lot of time, eg the car, or a friend's house. So when the mood takes you for a walk, you've no excuse!

My Prayer

Birthday wishes to a wife
*Another birthday, dear
Another day together
May you feel His presence near
Today, love, and forever.
Time has passed since we were young,
But you made my dreams come true,
May God be with you on this day
Because dear, I love you.*

Maureen E Todd-Davies, Swansea

✚YOUR GOOD HEALTH✚

Rise and shine

A good breakfast gives you the energy to get on with your morning. And if you're in a rush, that's no reason to miss out – try making a quick, nutrient-packed smoothie. Overnight, soak five dried prunes and eight dried apricots in a little water. In the morning, whiz them in the blender with 5tbsp plain live yoghurt and 8tbsp prune juice, and drink immediately. Crammed with fibre and immune-boosting antioxidant vitamins, it's a great start to your day.

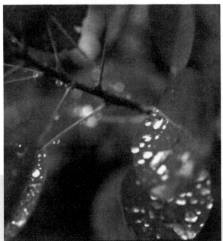

Plant of the week

Cotinus coggygria, the smoke bush, is a shapely rounded shrub and the variety 'Royal Purple' is popular for its lovely purple leaves which turn orange in autumn. In summer it's covered with a smoky haze of soft pinky flowers, which give it a smoke-like appearance. H3m (10ft)
● **Tip** – It can get quite large so prune it hard back in early spring.

And another thing...

Did you know that the easiest way to re-fold a road map is – differently.

A treasured memento

Marie and her daughter Jacqueline

In 1945, I was 13 years old and lived with my family at Thirsk.

Next door lived Mr and Mrs Wilkinson, son Derek and daughter Dora, always known as Dolly. Derek was in the Royal Navy and Dolly in Germany with the ATS.

When she came home she brought me a gold bracelet, with garnets.

She told us the German people at that time were living among the bomb sites, often in holes in the ground. Dolly had swapped food, chocolate and cigarettes for several pieces of jewellery, including this bracelet – many servicemen and women had done the same.

As I got older, and realised how heartbreaking this must have been, I have been torn between guilt for having this, and hope that whatever it was swapped for, was worth the sacrifice to the person concerned.

I do know that if I could have returned it, I would have done so, which is and always was, impossible. I have given it, along with this piece of history, to my daughter Jacqueline on her birthday.

Mrs Marie Jaques,
Scarborough

My Mum

Dorothy and her mum Kathleen on holiday

Here's my mum, Kathleen, doing what she likes best, soaking up the sun.

To celebrate her 90th birthday, my four sisters, myself, my two brothers and our partners took her to Gran Canaria. She'd never been abroad until she was in her 70s. Cnsidering her stout spirit, one wonders what she might like to do when she reaches 100!

Dorothy Jones, Bromsgrove

A treasured memento

I went on a school trip in 1953 to Kessingland in Norfolk for a week, and I bought a small gift for my parents – a large pebble painted with our holiday chalets on.

It was put away and probably forgotten about until 1981, when my parents died and house clearing began. I came across the stone again and it is now my treasure, as it was on that school holiday that my husband John and I started to enjoy each other's company (we were in the same class).

We'd met at 13, engaged at 18, married at 20 and now we've been married 45 years – and they said it couldn't last!

Jean Ross,
Warwickshire

Above: Jean and John
Left: Happy memories of Kessingland

✚YOUR GOOD HEALTH✚

Look after your legs

Did you know that 15 per cent of the population is plagued by restless leg syndrome, with older people most likely to be affected? This irritating condition causes tingling and an urge to move the legs, usually striking at night and disturbing sleep. Ease it by getting some activity during the day and having a hot bath in the evening. Avoid stimulants like caffeine and alcohol, and up your intake of iron-rich foods such as red meat and green leafy vegetables.

A RECIPE FOR YOU

Pear and Ginger Loaf Cake

- 225 g (8 oz) self raising flour
- 2 teaspoons ground ginger
- Pinch ground cloves
- $1/2$ teaspoon ground cinnamon
- Pinch of salt
- 175 g (6 oz) dark muscovado sugar
- 3 eggs, beaten
- 125 ml plain yoghurt
- 110 g (4 oz) butter, melted
- 2 large pears
- 50 g (2 oz) stem ginger, chopped

For the icing
- $1^1/2$ tablespoons ginger syrup from the jar
- 2-3 teaspoons hot water
- 110 g (4 oz) Golden Icing Sugar

1 Preheat the oven to 180°C, 350°F, Gas Mark 4. Grease and line a 1 lb (approx 400 g) loaf-tin.
2 Sift the flour, spices and salt into a mixing bowl. Add the sugar, eggs, yoghurt and butter, and stir until combined and the mixture is smooth.
3 Peel and thinly slice the pears and gently stir into the mixture with the stem ginger. Spoon into the prepared tin and bake for about $1^1/2$ hours until cooked through.
4 Cool in the tin for 10 minutes, then remove from the tin and transfer to a wire rack.
5 Sift the icing sugar into a bowl and gradually stir in the hot water and enough syrup to make an icing thick enough to coat the cake. Spoon over the top of the cold cake.

RECIPE COURTESY BILLINGTON'S

Run for it, lads!

During the Second World War I used to play Fag Cards in the street. We had to try and flick a card from a distance against those we'd stood up against a wall – and whoever knocked them down collected all the cards.

We'd play rounders, too, and even when there was an air-raid, we'd still play on. Until we heard a bomb whistling down – then we'd scarper indoors!

A bomb came down near our house and it blew the windows out of our house and our bedroom ceiling came down, too. The front door was left hanging on one hinge, so my mother and I had to clear it up because my dad was at work.

To earn my 6d pocket money, I worked at the local bakery, cleaning out the stables and feeding the three loveable shire horses. One of them trod on my foot with his back leg. I couldn't move, and he looked at me, and I swear he laughed.

Roy Durey, Maidstone, Kent

Plant of the week

Flowers don't come much more elegant than those of Zantedeschia aethiopica 'Crowborough' which has pure white hood-shaped blooms between late spring and mid-summer. It makes a striking architectural clump with lovely arrow-shaped, glossy dark green leaves. It looks great grown beside water as a marginal plant and can be left outside in most frost-prone areas if given a deep winter mulch. H90cm (3ft). AGM.

● **Tip** – If you haven't a pond, create a bog garden instead and grow it with other moisture-loving perennials.

Etiquette for Everybody
– 1920s' style –

On sitting in company…
'If you are bored, do not show it. Work hard to appear interested. Do not stare.'

TOP TIP

To reduce your fat intake, look for low-fat alternatives to your favourite foods – sausages, oven chips, yoghurts – all taste just as good!

And another thing...

GK Chesterton was so forgetful that he once got off a train and sent a telegram to his wife, 'Am in Market Harborough. Where ought I to be?'

My Mum

My Mum was a wonderful, kind, loving Mum, always there for me. She was a devout Christian, cared for my Dad, my Gran and I. She had a dicky heart, having had rheumatic fever as a child.

Among my many memories of her, I recall us both watching the wedding of Princess Margaret on television. Although neither of us knew it, she was gravely ill at the time and died soon afterwards at the young age of 64.

Margaret Exley,
Stourbridge

Left: Margaret today
Above: Margaret's mum on the right, with her sister May – they had a double wedding

Etiquette for Everybody
– 1920s' style –

On men & food…
'Somebody, who had more common sense than literary polish, once said that wives should 'Feed the brute.' There is a good deal in the saying. Meals and food have far more to do with peace of a home than a good many people would imagine.'

+YOUR GOOD HEALTH+

Going nutty

Chestnuts aren't just a fun plaything for schoolkids – they're high in vitamin B6, essential for keeping your brain sharp and your skin in good condition. So gather up some sweet chestnuts and roast them in the oven until they're soft enough to eat, or look out for the tinned version.

TOP TIP

Hang up your unwanted CDs at your window, to stop the birds from bumping into the glass. Sticking on black cut-out shapes of birds in flight can also act as a deterrent.

The day Freda lost her 'bottle'

Watching the VE Day reunions and celebrations last year brought back an embarrassing event for me. I was working at the City General Hospital in Leicester training to be a nurse in my first year, and I was very shy.

A message came through asking for a ward to be prepared for admission of soldiers from France, and I was allotted to the ward to prepare the beds. The soldiers arrived the next day, most were not serious cases but very pleased to be back in England again.

Junior Nurse Freda Church

As the junior nurse, I had the privilege of doing the 'bottle' round. I collected the metal pail full of urinals and gave them out one side of the ward, then a refill down the other side.

Then came the collection, down the first side, but at the last bed out came the urinal with a bunch of dandelions in the top! The last bottle didn't fit in the pail, so had to be carried. To make it worse, the men clapped my steps – I was scarlet!

Looking back, how wonderful it was that after all they had suffered, they could still play pranks! Can anyone recall that prank on the shy young Nurse Freda Church?

Freda R E Skelton, Leeds

Plant of the week

Echinacea purpurea is commonly called the cone flower and 'Magnus' is one of the most eye-catching varieties, producing large purple-pink flowers between June and September. Like other echinaceas, it's easy to grow and, being quite sturdy in nature, doesn't need staking. Echinaceas have enjoyed a surge in popularity thanks to the trend for naturalistic prairie-style planting schemes. Divide large clumps during the autumn. H75cm (30in).

● Tip – Plant echinaceas with other late summer-flowering plants such as asters and schizostylis.

My Prayer

God bless this little kitchen,
I love its every nook
And bless me as I do my work,
Wash pots and pans and cook.

And may the meals that I prepare
Be seasoned from above,
With Thy blessing and Thy grace,
But most of all Thy love.

As we partake of earthly food
The table for us spread.
We'll not forget to thank Thee, Lord,
Who gives us daily bread.

So bless my little kitchen, God
And those who enter in,
May they find naught but joy and peace
And happiness therein

Anon
Miss June V Bishop, Romford, Essex

A RECIPE FOR YOU

Sticky Sausages
(Serves 4)

● 1 tablespoon oil
● 12 sausages
● 150g (5 oz) dark muscovado sugar
● 50 ml (approx 2 fl oz) lemon juice
● 3 tablespoons sherry or ginger wine
● 3 tablespoons Seville or bitter orange marmalade
● 2 cloves garlic, crushed
● 2 tablespoons soy sauce
● Ground white pepper to taste

1 Heat the oil in a frying pan and brown the sausages on all sides. Drain off the fat and put the sausages into an ovenproof baking dish.
2 Put the remaining ingredients into a pan over a low heat and stir until the sugar has dissolved completely. Increase the heat and bring to the boil, then cook for 2-3 minutes.
3 Pour the sauce over the sausages. Cook for 10 minutes at 200°C, 400°F, Gas Mark 6, then baste with more sauce.
4 Cook for another 15-20 minutes until cooked through.

RECIPE COURTESY BILLINGTON'S

And another thing...

The top selling single of all time is Elton John's 1997 version of Candle in the Wind, followed by Bing Crosby's White Christmas, with Rock Around the Clock by Bill Haley and the Comets coming in third.

Wartime memories

Mrs Pat Butter of Solihull and her brothers and sisters were lucky to spend several years of the war living in a stately home

We were evacuated from North Finchley in London to Holkham Hall in Norfolk. Because there were six of us kids, Mum came with us. Another mother with six children was living in the same part of the house. Mum didn't have a pram for the baby so the lady at the big house gave us a very large elderly pram from their attic.

At night, we would open the ground-floor bedroom windows and the deer from the park would eat scraps of food from our hands. It was magical – we had never been that close to large animals before. We had some lovely picnics by the lake and walks in the woods but we were not allowed on the beach as it was mined and was protected by barbed wire.

There were soldiers billeted nearby so we were well looked after – the oldest children were driven to school in an army lorry. The soldiers also shared their rations with us. We had porridge every morning and a roast joint every Sunday.

During the school holidays, we had most of the grounds to play in. The gamekeepers' children told us naïve Londoners that if we ran after the pheasants and put salt on their tails we would be able to catch them. Needless to say, we never caught one.

I have only been back once, a couple of years ago. I didn't go into the Hall but this time I did go on the beach!

The photo shows both families, the Vachers (my family) and the Wadiloves, with Holkham Hall in the background. I'm the little girl next to the lady in the flowered dress, who is my Mum.

Keen to be green
Everyday ways to save the planet

- Boil only as much water as you need in a kettle – fill a cup or mug from the tap and pour this in to measure the precise amount.

- When buying new furniture, avoid pieces that are made from tropical hardwoods such as mahogany, teak, iroko or African walnut as these are all sourced from rainforests and have also had to be transported long distances.

- Don't overlook the obvious; insulating your hot water tank reduces heat loss by 75 per cent.

- Around the house, choose natural materials in preference to plastic eg a wicker waste-paper basket.

- A cut lemon is useful for removing tea stains from sinks and other surfaces. For other ways of avoiding the use of harsh chemical cleaners, visit websites www.greenshop.co.uk and www.naturalcollection.com.

- When you can, buy products such as washing-up liquid in refillable containers. The Body Shop will take old shampoo and conditioner bottles to be refilled (see website: www.thebodyshop.com).

- Don't be too hasty in throwing away old furniture, a local craftsmen may well be able to restore it to its former glory by gluing a broken leg or reupholstering it.

- Think of a nice, hot bath – which uses up to 20 gallons of water – as an occasional luxury and stick to a daily shower, which uses only six gallons of water.

- To save water when flushing the toilet, place a heavy object such as a brick in the cistern. Alternatively, use a plastic bottle that has been cut in half and filled with pebbles.

In the garden
- Scare the birds off your vegetable patch or allotment by hanging up old CDs and DVDs.

- Instead of throwing away the spent soil from used grow-bags, sprinkle it on the garden or add it to the compost heap.

Quiz

Test your knowledge with this fun quiz. If you get stuck the answers are at the bottom of the page.

1 In what year was the first pound coin introduced in Britain?

2 Approximately, how many pints of blood flow around an adult body?

3 What, according to the advertising slogan, were 'Naughty But Nice'?

4 Which long-running BBC variety show did Leonard Sachs host?

5 Which English seaside town is known as the English Riviera?

6 Who is the current host of the BBC's A Question Of Sport?

7 Clarinet maestro Acker Bilk is famous for wearing what on his head?

8 In the animal kingdom, approximately how long is the gestation period for an elephant?

9 Who caused widespread panic among millions of Americans in 1938, with his radio adaptation of H G Wells' War of the Worlds?

10 In which month does the Trooping of the Colour take place?

11 In which country would you be able to visit Sugarloaf Mountain?

12 Who wrote the novel Jamaica Inn?

Charles Laughton in Alfred Hitchcock's adaptation of Jamaica Inn

1 1983
2 8-10
3 Cream cakes
4 The Good Old Days
5 Torquay
6 Sue Barker
7 A bowler hat
8 22 months
9 Orson Welles
10 June
11 Brazil
12 Daphne du Maurier

An Autumn Whim

by Alan F Nicholls

Thirty years on, Terence still remembers the pretty teenager who first captured his heart

The business meeting had been a difficult one and Terence felt very tired even before he'd started the long drive home. It was a stormy autumn evening and the windscreen wipers were toiling under the combination of heavy rain and the spray thrown up by passing lorries. He calculated that it would be an hour before he reached the motorway and another two before he arrived home. Peering through the gloom, he saw a signpost indicating a turning ahead, Windlecombe 6.

Windlecombe! That was a name from the past. He hadn't been to Windlecombe for over 30 years. There had been a time, long ago, when he had passed through its narrow streets a couple of times a week. He remembered it as a pretty little Cotswold town with huddled mellow stone houses.

Terence grinned nostalgically as he remembered the greengrocer's shop in the main street and wondered, very doubtfully, if it was still there. He laughed to himself. Perhaps he should go and look! Well,

why not? It was Friday, there was no one waiting for him at home, and it was a filthy night. On a whim, he indicated left and turned on to the narrow road that took him the six miles to Windlecombe.

Even on a wet night, the little town seemed friendly and familiar. There should be a little hotel on the left. The Seven Stars, was it? Yes! Terence pulled into the car park, took his bag from the boot and walked through to the lounge bar. It was a welcoming room with an open log fire blazing in the hearth. Half a dozen people, obviously regulars, were exchanging banter across the bar.

Terence ordered a pint and asked the barmaid: "Do you have a room vacant for just one night's stay?"

The girl wasn't sure. "Wait one moment please, I'll get Elaine for you."

A couple of minutes later the door opened and a petite, attractive woman came through. She had beautifully-cut snow-white hair and clear, dark eyes. "Hallo, I'm Elaine. Kim tells me you're looking for

accommodation." Her warm smile took in his well-cut suit and expensive overnight bag. "Well, I think we can fit you in as long as you're not expecting the Hilton."

Terence followed Elaine upstairs and approved the small but comfortable bedroom. "Would you like a meal?" Elaine asked. "The special tonight is a fillet steak, stuffed with mussels, cooked in a red wine sauce. Our chef is rather good."

Terence said it certainly sounded as if the chef was rather good.

"About an hour then," she said, "if that's okay with you."

After she had gone Terence changed, then went out to look round the town. The rain had stopped but the pavements were still damp as he walked along the main street. A row of terraced houses had worn stone steps leading up to the front doors. This was where the greengrocer's shop had been but there was now no sign of it. He felt an unaccountable twinge of sadness, laughed at himself for the sentiment, and made his way back to The Seven Stars.

His table was ready, a bottle

> This was where the greengrocer's shop had been...

PIC: GETTY IMAGES

of red wine opened. When the pudding was served, Elaine came over to check that all was satisfactory and Terence asked her to sit and share a glass of wine with him.

"Tell me," he said, after they had exchanged pleasantries, "would you know what became of the little greengrocer's shop that used to be on the main street?"

Elaine looked puzzled. "Oh, you mean Turner's! That has been gone for 20 years. Why do you ask?"

"It's quite a silly story, really. When I was 19 I was in the RAF and I was stationed in Wiltshire. I used to cycle through Windlecombe on my way home to Birmingham every weekend. I always stopped at that greengrocer's to buy some

fruit. The girl who served me was about 16 – she was absolutely gorgeous and I was really smitten. I used to hang about outside the shop until I was sure that she was behind the counter, but I was always too shy to talk to her. Every week I would cycle along rehearsing irresistible chat up lines to impress her. Of course, when I got here, the words always froze on my lips and I would just ask for a couple of bananas or something."

Elaine laughed. "Ah yes, teenage love, I just about remember that!"

Terence continued: "This went on for the five months until I was posted overseas. I spent the whole week before my last leave psyching myself up, knowing it was my final

chance to get to know her. I had decided to ask her to write to me as my pen friend. On that last Saturday morning I went to the camp cycle shed to collect my bike only to find that it had been stolen, and I had to go home on the train."

Elaine stared at Terence for a moment: "That is quite extraordinary. I lived just a few doors down from Turner's and I knew your girl well. She was just the Saturday girl there and got a job in a building society after school. She eventually married a lovely man and they had two children. She and her husband, Dennis, bought a small hotel. Dennis died of cancer about ten years ago."

"That's sad," said Terence, "But I'm glad she had a happy married life. By the way, you never mentioned her name?"

She leaned over the table and said quietly: "Her name was Elaine."

Terence gaped, astonished, at her smiling face.

Elaine went on: "I used to pray every Friday night that you would pluck up the courage to talk about something except bananas. When I finally realised that you weren't going to come by any more, I cried for a week."

Recovering his senses, Terence said: "You really do have an excellent chef. Do you think I could stay for the weekend?"

October 2006

Sunday

1

Monday

2

Tuesday

3

Wednesday

4

Thursday

5

Friday

6

Saturday

7

Sunday

8

Monday

9

Tuesday

10

Wednesday

11

Yours October 11 issue on sale

Thursday

12

Friday

13

Saturday

14

Sunday

15

Monday

16

Tuesday

17

Wednesday

18

Thursday

19

Friday

20

Saturday

21

Sunday

22

Monday **23**	Saturday **28**
Tuesday **24**	Sunday **29** British Summer Time ends, clocks go back
Wednesday **25**	Monday **30**
Thursday **26**	Tuesday **31** Hallowe'en
Friday **27**	

Flavour of the month

October gives us, if we are lucky, a few more weeks of golden sunshine before British Summer Time ends on the twenty-ninth, but this month's real treasure is its golden leaves. In woods and gardens, autumn bows out in a glorious blaze of russet, amber and palest yellow.

Youngsters abandon their computer games to search among the fallen leaves for gleaming chestnuts to play conkers, as their fathers and grandfathers did before them. At the end of the month boys and girls will be dressing up as witches and ghosts and ringing doorbells for 'trick or treat' so it is a good idea to have a few sweets and chocolates ready to hand out.

The evenings are chilly now and it is time to prepare for the colder months to come by ordering fuel for the central heating and, if you have an old-fashioned open fire, laying up a good store of logs and coal. There is every chance of frosts at night and gardeners need to move tender plants into the shelter of a greenhouse or conservatory. Dahlias should not be dug up until the first frosts have blackened the foliage.

With the longer evenings, our thoughts turn once again to indoor pursuits. Now is the time to get out those knitting needles and knit yourself a pretty jumper. If you fancy taking up a different hobby, see what is available at your local evening classes. Or visit the library and indulge in the luxury of curling up with a good book.

PIC: HENRYK T. KAISER/REX FEATURES

My Mum

This photograph is one of my Mother and I taken at the Exhibition on the London embankment in 1951. It's from one of my old photograph albums where it had been put with others all entitled 'Smiler and Me'.

My Mother was a real character, who was always ready to help people. She wasn't just my Mother but my friend and was the one person who understood how I felt when I failed the eleven plus.

She was an expert seamstress who made a lot of her own clothes My three daughters became good needlewomen, too. I think it skipped a generation because I'm absolutely hopeless!

On the day we spent at the Exhibition, Dad had disappeared off on his own but he must have returned to take the photograph, as we strolled around, arm in arm, both with grins on our faces, like two schoolchildren playing truant…

Jean Clark, Exmouth

Jean and her mum in 1951

A treasured memento

I was born at the beginning of October 1939, not long after the Second World War broke out. Soon after my birth my father left to serve in the army so I didn't see him again until I was six.

While he was away, my Mother and I spent most of our time with my aunt and uncle who ran a fish and chip shop.

My aunt and uncle had no children and Uncle Jim was my father figure – I adored him. If Mum and Auntie Emma were ever annoyed with me, he'd say, 'Come on love, put your coat on – we'll go out.' He'd carry me for miles on his shoulders.

Mum and I used to go on holiday with them to Blackpool and Uncle Jim taught me to swim. I didn't see my father for years, although 'Daddy' was always talked about and when I went to Sunday School, and we had Bible texts to colour in, Mum used to say, 'Colour it neatly to send to Daddy.'

However, when the war was over and Daddy returned home, we had a difficult relationship but as the years went by we grew closer. In my early teens, Uncle Jim bought me a heart-shaped silver locket I wanted, which I always wore. Sadly, he died just before I took my A-levels. However, I had my locket and even wore it for my wedding in 1967. I don't wear it any longer but would never part with it, and I look at it often.

Mrs Barbara Cox, Northumberland

Above: Barbara on her wedding day
Right: Barbara today

Plant of the week

Rudbeckias, which have yellow daisy-like flowers with dark centres, are commonly called black-eyed Susan and are a great late-summer perennial. They thrive in sun or partial shade and will cope in most soils as long as they're not waterlogged. The large, single, yellow flowers of rudbeckias have made it a popular choice among gardeners, and there are also doubles and compact varieties in the family. They all have a long flowering season, spreading sunshine in your borders between mid-summer and late autumn. The height of the plant depends on its variety and may range between 30cm (1ft) and 1.8m (6ft).

● **Tip** – Try the annual varieties of rudbeckia if you want a quick display next spring.

And another thing...

Did you know that in still conditions, a thrush can be heard nearly a mile away?

+YOUR GOOD HEALTH+

Step out!
We should all be aiming to take 10,000 steps a day to keep our hearts healthy, says the British Heart Foundation – but most of us manage less than 5,000. So invest in a cheap pedometer (from department stores and chemists) and make the most of beautiful crisp autumn days by going for brisk strolls in your nearest park. That step count will soon mount up!

A RECIPE FOR YOU

Golden Almond and Apple Tart
(Serves 8)

● 75 g (3 oz) Golden Caster Sugar, plus 1 tablespoon
● 75 g (3 oz) butter
● 75 g (3 oz) ground almonds
● 2 large eggs, beaten
● 1 cooked 20 cm (8 inch) pastry case
● 1 red apple
● 1 green apple
● 2 tablespoons lemon juice
● 150 ml (¼ pint) double or whipping cream
● 1 tablespoon golden icing sugar

1 Cream the Golden Caster Sugar with the butter until light.
2 Beat in the ground almonds and eggs. Spoon into the pastry case, spreading out evenly.
3 Core the apples and slice them thinly. Toss in the lemon juice and arrange on top of the almond mixture.
4 Sprinkle with the remaining Golden Caster Sugar.
5 Bake for about 25 minutes at 180°C, 350°F, Gas Mark 4 until firm. Cool slightly.
6 Whip the cream and Golden Icing Sugar until thick and serve with the tart.
● This recipe contains nuts   RECIPE COURTESY BILLINGTON'S

TOP TIP

Take old catalogues into your local playschool, to see if they can be used for 'cutting and glueing'.

And another thing...

'Let us be thankful for the fools. But for them the rest of us could not succeed.'
Mark Twain

My Prayer

My late husband, John, bought me a beautifully crafted and matted version of this from a craft shop in Florida. I have always done crafts and flower arranging and he would tease me about keeping the dining table covered with my current project – and having to have our meal in the kitchen or on a tray.

A Crafter's Prayer
*I love to paint and glue and sew
And decorate with laces
Make wooden toys and ornaments
With smiling, painted faces.*

*Lord, when I've risen from the dead
And before Your throne I stand
I'll have a halo on my head,
A home-made craft in my hand.*

*I never learned to sing or play
So let no harp be mine
From childhood to my dying day
Crafting will be my line.*

*My closets are bursting
with ribbon and yarn
And boxes of scraps galore
I fear my mate will leave me if
I gather any more.*

*I pray that when I die
And to Heaven I arise
You'll grant me just one last request
May I bring my craft supplies?*
Anon
Margery Utley, Chelmsford

Plant of the week

Heleniums are another late summer beauty which should be included in every planting scheme. The majority of varieties have daisy-like flowers in shades of orange, yellow and red but if you have to choose one, it should be 'Moerheim Beauty', which is one of the best with flame-coloured flowers. Divide large clumps during the autumn as this will maintain vigour. H90cm (3ft).
● **Tip** – Plant in large groups to creat a swathe of colour.

TOP TIP

When dusting the television screen, use an old pastry brush to get the static out of the corners.

A treasured memento

I hold in the palm of my hand, a small, very dry and fragile palm leaf. On it is written, in mauve pencil:
'*Best wishes from Durban
Love from Henry, April 3, 1917.*'
My father sent this to my mother, while he was serving in the Royal Engineers in the First World War. Nothing would make me part with this; it still gives out such love after all these years.
Edna M Wilde, Worcester

Etiquette for Everybody
– 1920s' style –

On guests...
'All ideas of gushing must be avoided. The visitor whose superlatives are as numerous as the grains of sand on the seashore is a person whom nobody respects.

A RECIPE FOR YOU

Lamb and Vegetable Crumble
(Serves 4)

- 450 g (1 lb) lean minced lamb
- 15 ml (1 tablespoon) oil
- 1 stick celery, finely chopped
- 2 medium onions, peeled and finely chopped
- 2 carrots, peeled and diced
- 1 sprig fresh rosemary, finely chopped
- 30 ml (2 tablespoons) plain flour
- 30 ml (2 tablespoons) tomato purée
- 45 ml (3 tablespoons) Worcestershire sauce
- 425 ml (approx ¾ pint) lamb stock
- 1 can (approx 198g) sweetcorn

For the crumble
- 75 g (3 oz) plain wholemeal flour
- 75 g (3oz) plain flour
- 75 g (3 oz) butter
- 100 g (4 oz) grated mature Cheddar cheese
- 30-45 ml (2-3 tablespoons) freshly chopped chives

1 Heat the oil in a large pan and cook the minced lamb over a moderate heat until brown. Add the celery, onions and carrots, and cook for 5 minutes. Add the rosemary.

2 Stir in 30 ml (2 tablespoons) plain flour, the tomato purée, Worcestershire sauce, lamb stock and season. Bring to the boil and reduce the heat. Add the drained can of sweetcorn.

3 Spoon the mixture into a 1.2 L (approx 2 pt) ovenproof dish or four 300 ml (approx ½ pt) individual dishes.

4 Meanwhile, place 75 g (3 oz) plain wholemeal flour and the 75 g (3 oz) plain flour into a large bowl. Rub in the butter until the mixture resembles fine breadcrumbs. Stir in the cheese and the chives.

5 Spoon the crumble on top of the meat and bake at 180°C, 350°F, Gas Mark 5, for 25-30 minutes if using one dish, or for 15-20 minutes if using four dishes, until bubbling.

RECIPE COURTESY THE ENGLISH BEEF AND LAMB EXECUTIVE

A whirlwind romance

Joy and Ashley on their wedding day in 1944

I was 17 years old and Ashley, my late husband was 19 when he asked me to dance and – Wham! – that was it! We married on January 15, 1944, with three days honeymoon in Torquay.

He was Petty Office Shouler on HMS Harrier, the leading minesweeper on Russian convoys, and I, Private Joy Jerham, ATS Signals.

He died in 1990 leaving me heartbroken; I still have hundreds of letters from him.

Joy Shouler, Lancing, West Sussex

✚YOUR GOOD HEALTH✚

Colour up
Colour therapists believe different shades can affect our wellbeing.
If you're...
- Exhausted – try wearing yellow, or buy yourself a big bunch of yellow flowers
- Depressed – add a touch of uplifting orange to your outfit
- Stressed – soothing green is your best bet – take a walk in your nearest area and focus on the trees and grass

A race against time

Left: Thorney floods, 1947. Right: Julie (back) and Betty with some Suffolk Punch horses

I remember the floods in the Fenlands in 1947. I was in the Land Army at Thorney and we were told there were floods in Crowland. The foreman at Gores Farm, Whittlesey Road, sent us land girls to help the farmer get his potatoes up from a potato grave, ready to be moved by lorry to a safer place.

While we were working, we could see the flood water getting nearer to us, but we still had to carry on. One morning our hostel warden told us not to go the farm as the flood water had arrived.

My next job was with my friend Julie, outside the German POW camp in Thorney, making corned beef sandwiches and tea for the lorry drivers who were taking the POWs to help with the floods.

Betty Spridgeon, Whittlesey, Peterborough

✚YOUR GOOD HEALTH✚

Beat the blues

The lethargy and depression linked with Seasonal Affective Disorder (SAD) affects at least half a million of us, with many more experiencing milder symptoms of the winter blues. Daily exposure to intense light helps in 85 per cent of cases, so if the colder months are a struggle for you, it could be worth investing in a light therapy box, which simulates natural daylight. Light treatment is most effective if you start using it before the days grow shorter. For an information pack on SAD treatments, send £5 to: The Administrator, SAD Association, PO Box 989, Steyning, BN44 3HG.

A RECIPE FOR YOU

Beef and Beer Casserole with Caraway Seed Dumplings

(Serves 4)

- 450 g (approx 1 lb) lean beef cubes
- 1 tablespoon sunflower oil
- 100 g (4 oz) streaky bacon, cubed
- 1 large clove garlic, peeled and crushed
- 10-12 shallots, peeled
- 225 g (8 oz) baby carrots, peeled
- 225 g (8 oz) baby turnips, peeled
- 2 tablespoons plain flour
- 600 ml (1 pint) stout or brown ale
- Salt and freshly milled black pepper
- 3-4 fresh thyme sprigs
- 2 fresh bay leaves

For the caraway seed dumplings:
- 175 g (6 oz) self-raising flour
- 75 g (3 oz) butter, cubed
- 1-2 teaspoons caraway seeds
- 3-4 tablespoons water

1 Preheat the oven to 170°C, 325°F, Gas Mark 3.
2 Heat the oil in a large pan and cook the meat for 4-5 minutes, in batches until brown. Add the bacon and fry for 3-4 minutes, stirring until the bacon is crispy.
3 Transfer to a large casserole dish and add the garlic, shallots, carrots and turnips. Stir in the plain flour and cook for 1-2 minutes.
4 Pour over the stout or brown ale, bring to the boil and reduce the heat. Season and add the fresh herbs. Cover and cook for 1½-2 hours or until the meat is tender.
5 **Prepare dumplings:** Rub the butter into the self-raising flour to make fine breadcrumbs. Season. Add the caraway seeds and water. Mix together to form a smooth dough. Shape into 10-12 small balls.
6 20 minutes before the end of cooking, add the dumplings to the casserole, return to the oven and cook uncovered for the remaining cooking time.

RECIPE COURTESY QUALITY STANDARD BEEF AND LAMB

Plant of the week

Choisya ternata is commonly called Mexican orange blossom and the variety 'Sundance' is a great low maintenance shrub quickly reaching 1.5m (5ft) in height. Evergreen, it really stands out in the garden all year round due to its attractively-coloured leaves. Although it doesn't flower as profusely as C. ternata and its fragrant white flowers look strange against the leaves, it's worth growing for its leaves alone. It thrives in sun or shade, but looks most attractive in shade because the leaves become a vibrant lime-green colour. It will grow in most soils as long as they're not waterlogged.

● Tip – Prune it hard back in mid summer if it's outgrowing its space.

And another thing...

'A woman rang to say she heard there was a hurricane on the way. Well, don't worry, there isn't'
Michael Fish on the night before serious gales in southern England.

My Mum

Here is an extract from Audrey's tribute to her Mum:

Dear Mum -
I remember all the happy times
And your loving, gentle touch…

I went through a phase of arguing
As most teenagers do
And thought mostly about myself
With not much thought for you.

But you were always there for me
And forgave me any pain
That I must have put you through
And we'd be friends again.

You listened to my tales of woe
And gave me good advice,
You vetted all my boyfriends
And told me who were nice.

Audrey's mum by the sea

But later when I married
And had my children too
I knew just what it felt like
To be a Mum like you.

I knew then just how much you cared
And I hoped that I'd become
Just by your fine example
A wise and loving mum.

Mrs Audrey Harris, Charlton

Audrey today

Etiquette for Everybody
– 1920s' style –

On husbands…
'Make a fuss of him on his birthday, and when he is ill give him lots of sympathy. Most men like sympathy.'

October 23-29

TOP TIP

Don't throw that old bit of carpet away – use it as a kneeler when weeding in the garden.

A treasured memento

My treasured mementos are two photographs of myself and my mother in London, one at Horse Guards' Parade and the other at the Tower of London. They were taken in 1948 by my father when I was eight years old. We used to go up to London a lot and I loved it.

Thelma E Bailey, West Drayton

Above: Thelma and her mother on Horse Guards' Parade
Right: Outside the Tower of London

A RECIPE FOR YOU

Bramley and Walnut Scones
(Makes 9)

- 225 g (8 oz) self-raising flour
- 5 ml (1 teaspoon) baking powder
- 50 g (2 oz) butter
- 225 g (8 oz) Bramley apples, peeled, cored and chopped
- 4 tablespoons caster sugar
- 25 g (1 oz) walnut pieces, chopped
- 150 ml (¼ pt) milk, plus a little to glaze

To serve:
- Bramble jam
- Clotted cream

1 Preheat the oven to 220°C, 425°F, Gas Mark 7.
2 Sift the flour and baking powder together into a bowl. Rub in the butter until the mixture resembles crumbs.
3 Stir in the apples, sugar and walnuts; then stir in enough of the milk to mix to a soft dough.
4 Roll out the mixture on a floured surface until it is 5 cm (2 ins) thick. Press out 9 rounds using a 6 cm (2½ ins) round fluted cutter. Place well apart on a baking sheet, brush the tops with the remaining milk.
5 Bake for 10-15 mins or until golden and risen. Cool on a wire rack. Serve split, spread with butter or topped with jam and clotted cream.
- This recipe contains nuts

RECIPE COURTESY OF BRAMLEY APPLE INFORMATION SERVICE

Memories of childhood

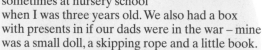

I remember having to wear a Mickey Mouse gas mask sometimes at nursery school when I was three years old. We also had a box with presents in if our dads were in the war – mine was a small doll, a skipping rope and a little book.

When I was older, I used to do French knitting with an old cotton reel and four nails. I also liked to go butterflying with my net, and I can remember earning pocket money by picking hips and doing the shopping for an elderly lady.

There were lots of American soldiers around and one of them, Arthur, brought me a little khaki drawstring bag full of sweets and chewing gum. I later used it as a plimsoll bag.

Jill Sharp, Northampton

And another thing...

'Fancy being remembered around the world for the invention of a mouse!'   *Walt Disney*

My Prayer

For those who feel alone
*I feel alone dear Lord, so stay by my side
In all my daily needs, be Thou my guide.
Grant me good health, for that indeed I pray
To carry on my work, from day to day.*

*Keep pure my mind, my thoughts, my every deed
Let me be kind, unselfish in my neighbour's need.
Spare me from fire, from flood, and malicious tongues
From thieves, from fear and evil ones.*

*If sickness or an accident befall,
Then humbly, Lord, I pray, hear Thou my call,
And when I'm feeling low or in despair,
Lift up my heart and help me in my prayer.
I feel alone dear Lord, yet have no fear,
Because I feel your presence ever near!*

Audrey Faul, Hartlepool

Plant of the week

When it comes to bathrooms, a tradescantia is one of the best plants you can choose with waxy variegated leaves that look attractive all year round. It loves a humid warm atmosphere and will quickly trail over the edges of its basket. Keep the compost moist during the growing season – you can let it dry out a little during the winter and give a weak liquid feed weekly during the summer.
● **Tip** – Encourage the stems to twine upwards around the chains of the basket.

Etiquette for Everybody
– 1920s' style –

On reading...
'If a wife has time to read, it should not be novels and nothing but novels. The morning papers and intelligent magazines should not be ignored. They will help to keep her mind fresh and alert.'

Wartime memories

Mrs Violet Bandey of Bures in Suffolk never let go of her sister Freda's hand when they were evacuated to Wales

My sister Freda was five years old when my parents were told that she was going to be evacuated. I was aged four and they would not let her go unless I went, too. We had always been together and they felt that we would be a support for one another in our new home.

My parents had always dressed us alike and they bought us new winter coats, hats, socks and shoes in the hope that these would help us go to a 'good' home. "Stay together – don't let go of each other's hands," they told us.

I fell asleep on the long train journey and when Freda started fidgeting, one of the teachers in charge of us asked her what was the matter. Freda explained that she needed to go to the toilet but she could not go down the corridor without letting go of my hand. She waited until I woke up!

On arriving at St Mellon's, a small village about ten miles from Cardiff, we were taken to a classroom where a lady sat at the high teacher's desk. In front of the desk was a queue of people who pointed at a child and said: "I'll have that one."

It all seemed to take ages. When I looked round, the room was almost empty and I burst into tears. "Nobody wants us!" I cried but everyone laughed because it turned out that the lady who was taking down the names and addresses, Mrs Birchall, had put us against her name right at the beginning. She thought we were twins.

Mr and Mrs Birchall had a very nice home and we came to know them as our St Mellon's mummy and daddy. After a few years, when my parents came to visit us, we all went for a walk. Freda walked along holding hands with them but I walked behind with Mr and Mrs Birchall because I was shy of my own parents.

♻ Keen to be green Everyday ways to save the planet

Six ideas for using old newspapers:
- Use to line the car boot when transporting rubbish to the tip or plants from the garden centre.
- Dampen and spread over window panes before painting the frames.
- Shred and use for packing fragile items.
- Stuff in the crown of hats to keep their shape in storage.
- Fold into strips to use as firelighters.
- Stuff in wet shoes to dry overnight.

- Re-use pump-top dispensers for handwash by filling them with liquid detergent.

- Having your milk delivered helps to minimise waste because dairies wash and re-use glass bottles.

- Whenever possible, use rechargeable batteries instead of disposable ones.

- If you have a home computer, only print out items that you really need to keep and try to print on both sides of the paper, if you can.

- When you go for a walk, take a plastic carrier bag with you to pick up litter and dispose of it in a litter bin or in your own dustbin when you get home.

- If there isn't already a paper recycling scheme at your place of work, why not start one.

In the garden
- Collect ash from bonfires while it is still dry to sprinkle round fruit trees as a source of potash.

- Wrap green tomatoes in newspaper to ripen.

- If you win a coconut at the fair, break up the shell and spread it around plants as a slug and snail deterrent – they don't like crawling over sharp edges.

Test your knowledge with this fun quiz. If you get stuck the answers are at the bottom of the page.

PIC: REX FEATURES

1 In what year was the Mary Rose raised from the bottom of the Solent, where it had sunk in 1545?

2 Arthur Mullard starred in which 1976 sitcom alongside Queenie Watts and Mike Reid?

3 Who played Purdy in The New Avengers?

4 According to the words of Benny Hill's novelty number one hit, Ernie (The Fastest Milkman In The West), what were heard rattling in their crates?

5 Lincoln is the capital city of which US state?

6 John Steinbeck wrote which notable novel?

7 Which sport would you associate brothers Graham and Martin Bell?

8 In George Orwell's novel 1984, who is said to be watching you?

9 After appearing on which TV talent show in the 1970s did Lena Zavaroni shoot to fame?

10 Roger De Courcey worked with which famous puppet?

11 Who is The Maid of Orleans more commonly known as?

12 Jack Regan and George Carter were characters in which hugely popular TV police drama of the 1970s?

1 1982
2 Yus My Dear
3 Joanna Lumley
4 Ernies ghostly goldtops
5 Nebraska
6 Of Mice And Men
7 Downhill skiing
8 Big Brother
9 Opportunity Knocks
10 Nookie Bear
11 Joan of Arc
12 The Sweeney

A postcard from

Minarets sparkling in the sun, spice markets and fish fresh from the sea. There was all this and more for Wyn Terret, as she travelled to Istanbul for a family celebration...

"**H**ello Mum, I've decided to have a 40th birthday party here in Istanbul before we leave as we've got another posting for the next two years."

It was my daughter Claire ringing from Turkey where she, her husband Tim and three children, James, Alexandra and Holly had been posted for the last four years. I sat there stunned by this as they were due to return to England in July for good.

"Mum, are you okay?"

"I'll be fine love, just give me time to get used to the idea, now tell me about this party…"

Claire's excited voice rushed on. It was wonderful to hear her. It seemed only a short while ago, that she had stood on a balcony watching the bombs explode over the city, not

knowing if Tim was alive or dead.

One month later, my husband Stan and I, together with other members of the family, arrived in Istanbul. The sun sparkled on the Bosphorus, the skyline was etched with domed mosques, and minarets pointed up to a blue sky like sharpened pencils.

First stop, the spice market which was a riot of colour and smells. Pashminas of every hue mingled with china, jewellery, exotic spices and Turkish Delight flavoured with nuts, fruit, rose and lemon. "Taste before you buy madam," which we did with great alacrity, each equally delicious with every stall we passed. It was strange to hear Claire speaking Turkish. All the children can make themselves understood, but I learned 'tesekkurler', meaning

thank you, and 'gule gule', goodbye, but literally meaning, go smiling, which I thought delightful.

We all enjoyed the trip on the Bosphorus, setting off with 20 others in a small boat in brilliant sunshine. Then, amid the clink of glasses, a backdrop of a tangerine sunset and smells of sizzling chicken coming from the galley, the sun went down and on came all the twinkling lights from the houses built into the hillside. We passed several wedding boats with the bride and groom dancing on the deck before it was time to moor at the halfway point. The lights and the engine were switched off.

There was absolute silence for several minutes, to be broken by a muffled voice saying, 'This is where they ask us for ransom money.' We all laughed and the romantic moment passed.

The following day we had lunch at a local fish restaurant set down a cobbled street. Once seated, we were shown a large platter containing an assortment of fish, complete with heads and staring eyes. After choosing our fish, and while we waited for them to be cooked, an elderly man with a face like tanned leather

Turkey

Above: The mosques and minarets of Istanbul
Left: The heady smells of the spice market
Below, left: Turkish ladies making pancakes, or 'gazleme'
Below: The Cistern, cool serenity under the streets of Istanbul

approached our table offering to clean our shoes. He returned them in pristine condition for fifty pence.

Opposite was a man lighting his coal stove beneath a column of meat, sharpening his knives in readiness for his customers asking for a doner kebab. The man carrying simits, (large rings of special bread covered in sesame seeds) in a huge pyramid on a basket on top of his head, gave us a cheery wave as he passed us, as we demolished our delicious fish.

On the way home the children told us that we'd be going to see their school the following day, as it was their Family Fun Day, (just like our school fête.) Our two eldest grandchildren go to the British International School. With only 12 children, they mix easily with all nationalities and learn readily in such small classes. Even the youngest, Holly, loves nursery school where all the other children are Turkish but language seems to present no problems for her.

Once inside the gate on Fun Day, we saw a Turkish lady sitting on the ground in front of a round flat stone pressing out large pancakes called gazleme which another lady cooked. The soft fruit toffee twists on a stick, were very 'moreish' and cooked by a man in old Ottoman costume. The stalls contained a variety of things including embroidered cushions, Turkish jewellery – and English paperbacks which were at a premium, as was the marmalade and lemon curd!

The day of the party arrived and did we work hard. The ladies cooked and chopped, the men climbed ladders to hang fairy lights in trees, pushed in flares to line the paths and put up tables decorated with flowers, candles, oranges and lemons. The sun went down, we dressed up, the stage was set.

"How many are coming?" I asked Claire. "We're not actually sure as many Turkish people just arrive."

"I hope they do," I answered, looking at the mountains of food.

We needn't have worried – 120 guests arrived! Tim was presented with a leaving gift of a pair of fragile Turkish tea cups in a red velvet box and a plaque.

"Mum," said Claire, taking me to one side at the end of the evening, "this has been a truly magical evening. Thanks so much for coming, it just wouldn't have been the same without you all."

On the last morning of our holiday we drove to the seaside for coffee. We sat chatting, while the children stared at a glass tank full of fish. What a wonderful holiday to remember.

November 2006

Wednesday

1
All Saints' Day

Thursday

2
Order **Yours** subscriptions now for Christmas

Friday

3

Saturday

4

Sunday

5
Bonfire Night

Monday

6

Tuesday

7

Wednesday

8
Yours November 8 issue on sale

Thursday

9

Friday

10

Saturday

11

Sunday

12
Remembrance Sunday

Monday

13

Tuesday

14

Wednesday

15

Thursday

16

Friday

17

Saturday

18

Sunday

19

Monday

20

Tuesday

21

Wednesday

22

Thursday	Monday
23	27
Friday	Tuesday
24	28
Saturday	Wednesday
25	29
Sunday	Thursday
26	30
First Sunday of Advent	St Andrew's Day

Flavour of the month

Not many people count foggy November as their favourite month but most of us are too busy with early Christmas preparations to be cast down by gloomy days. November 26 is Stir Up Sunday when everyone in the family takes a turn at giving the plum pudding mixture a good stir and makes a wish.

Tidying the garden is another November occupation, piling up the rubbish that can't be composted to make a bonfire to burn the guy on November 5. The tradition of lighting a bonfire at this time of the year goes back long before Guy Fawkes – the Druids lit fires to mark the beginning of the winter solstice.

Whatever the weather, Londoners turn out on the second Saturday of the month to enjoy the spectacle of the Lord Mayor's Show, which was first held in 1215. They also loyally line the streets to cheer the Queen on her way to the ceremonial opening of Parliament.

As well as pageantry, November offers occasions for quiet contemplation and recollection. On All Souls' Day, which falls on the second of the month, it is customary to spend time praying for the souls in purgatory. On November 11, Armistice Day, we pause to remember in silence all those brave service men and women who gave their lives for their country.

Tulip bulbs should not be planted until late autumn to reduce the risk of Botrytis blight, so now is the time to put them in the ground and look forward to enjoying their splendid colours next spring.

My Mum

My Mother Eleanor Julia was nicknamed Nellie from an early age. She was born in 1904 and lived at Hall Farm, Heston, which is now beneath Heathrow Airport. It wasn't crops she was interested in, but the animals, horses in particular – she was a true farm lover.

Very soon, my mother learned to drive the pony and trap; she loved Polly, her pony. Years later, the family moved to Applegarth, Ashford, a detached house with a large garden and my mother was thrilled when they kept chickens – Mickey the dog arrived, too.

We moved to Sunningdale

Left: Eleanor (right) at Hall Farm, Heston, with Polly the pony in the 1920s
Right: Eleanor with Priscilla at Applegarth in 1937

before the war but were in Ashford when the Second World War broke out, and it was 1942 before we had our own home again. Immediately, Mother wanted a pet cat and some chickens for eggs. Fee-Fee was the perfect black and white cat who kept us company in the shelter during the air raids.

With peace in 1945 came Dusty, Fee-Fee's kitten and when Dusty died Mother was heartbroken. Throughout her life, Mother adored animals. There were none in her last years, in residential care, so she watched the birds from her bedroom window. She loved all creatures, great and small.

Priscilla O'Dell,
Hampton, Middx

A treasured memento

Around 20 years ago my late husband bought me a keyring – a little train, and when you press the chimney, the sound of it chugging along and the whistle blowing is very real.

When my husband was ill and couldn't climb the stairs, I kept it on the shelf in the hall by the telephone and when I went to bed after settling him for the night, I used to press the chimney to activate the train. I'd do the same thing in the morning to let him know I was around.

Although he's no longer with me, I still have the train, which still chugs along – a real treasure.

Ivy Wood, Brecon

TOP TIP

Taking fruit and salad vegetables out of the fridge a while before you need them helps bring out their flavour, to say nothing of being kinder on the teeth!

Etiquette for Everybody
– 1920s' style –

On manners...
'Talking loudly in public vehicles is not a sign of aristocracy; it is a nuisance to people who want to read.'

Plant of the week

If you're always killing houseplants then try a peace lily or spathiphyllum instead – it's an extremely resilient plant and some would say it thrives on neglect. The white flowers, which are actually bracts look great above the dark green leaves. You can buy spathiphyllums in flower all year round and they make great presents. Place them in a cool bright place and ensure the compost remains moist.

● **Tip** – When the plant requires repotting only move it up one pot size as restricting the roots slightly encourages flowering.

And another thing...

'Music is everybody's possession. Only publishers think that people own it'.

John Lennon

✚YOUR GOOD HEALTH✚

Get your vitamins

A vegetable juice is a great way to boost your vitamin intake. Try one with beetroot and kale, both excellent for cleansing your system. Juice three carrots, half an apple, half an orange, a quarter of a beetroot, one stick of celery, and two large kale leaves. Drink immediately – it tastes sweeter than it sounds!

A RECIPE FOR YOU

Roast Trout with Horseradish Sauce

(Serves 4)

● 700 g (1½ lb) new potatoes, finely sliced
● 2 garlic cloves, finely sliced
● 1 onion finely sliced
● 4 tablespoon olive oil
● Sea salt and ground black pepper
● 4 whole trout, gutted
● Handful rosemary sprigs
● 1 lemon, finely sliced
● 50 g (2 oz) bacon lardons
● 1 small tub crème fraîche
● 3 tbsp creamed horseradish

1 Place a layer of potatoes in a large roasting tin, sprinkle over the garlic and onion slices, 3 tablespoons olive oil and season well. Cook at 200°C, 400°F, Gas Mark 6 for 15 minutes.

2 Rinse the trout under a running tap and pat dry. Season the insides of the trout and stuff with 2-3 sprigs of rosemary and some lemon slices. Rub with the remaining olive oil and season with sea salt flakes and ground black pepper.

3 Remove the tin from the oven and arrange the trout on the potatoes and top with the bacon lardons and any remaining rosemary sprigs, return to the oven for a further 10-15 minutes.

4 Meanwhile, bring the crème fraîche to the boil in a small pan, bubble until reduced by half, then add the horseradish sauce. Serve the trout with the potatoes and crispy bacon, and warm sauce.

RECIPE COURTESY THE BRITISH TROUT ASSOCIATION

A treasured memento

My precious memento is a poem written by my father, Joseph Rayment, who was a leading cook on HMS Ibis in World War Two. I was born on October 1, 1941 and my father paid the ultimate sacrifice on November 10, 1942, so I can't remember him. My brother was born in June 1942 and the line which says 'soon will come our tiny son' must have been wishful thinking as a letter to him saying my mother was pregnant was returned unopened after he was killed. The poem is about me and my mother (who was Joan Brenda) but my father's pet name for her was Bobby.

Here is an extract:

'To my darling wife Bobby
and precious daughter, Ann
The Atlantic seas are rising
The waning sun grows red
I close my eyes a moment
And somehow I see instead
My wife and baby Ann so dear
While I have them I know no fear.

I know that I must fight, and yet
My wife and babe I'll not forget
So far Ann is our only one
But soon will come our tiny son.'

Mrs Ann Horner, St Neot's, Cambs

Left: Ann's father Joseph in navy uniform
Right: Ann with her dog

PIC: GARDEN PICTURE LIBRARY/IKEA

Plant of the week

Calatheas are extraordinarily beautiful houseplants with spectacular leaves. They make great specimens but are unsuitable for the garden, needing a minimum temperature of around 17C. They require bright but not direct sunlight, high levels of humidity and an absence of draughts.

● **Tip** – Choose a container which matches the colour of the markings on the leaves and you'll create extra impact.

TOP TIP

Don't be caught out if the power goes. Always keep a torch somewhere easy to get to in the dark, and candles and matches in a convenient place.

Etiquette for Everybody
– 1920s' style –

On children...
'Remember that healthy children must be a little noisy.'

And another thing...

'Be pleased to remember that there are bright stars under the most palpable clouds, and light is never so beautiful as in the presence of darkness.' *Henry Vaughan, poet*

A RECIPE FOR YOU

Cornish Black Cake

- 175 g (6 oz) raisins
- 175 g (6 oz) sultanas
- 75 g (3 oz) candied peel, chopped
- 8 tablespoons stout
- 175 g (6 oz) butter
- 175 g (6 oz) molasses sugar
- 3 medium eggs, beaten
- 225 g (8 oz) plain flour
- 1 teaspoon ground mixed spice
- 1 teaspoon ground cinnamon
- 75 g (3 oz) blanched almonds, chopped

1 Place the dried fruits and peel in a bowl and pour over the stout. Cover and leave to stand overnight.
2 Preheat the oven to 150°C, 300°F, Gas Mark 2.
3 Cream the butter and sugar until smooth, then beat in the eggs a little at a time.
4 Sift in the flour and spices and fold into the mixture with the soaked fruit and any remaining liquid. Stir in the almonds. The mixture should be of a soft dropping consistency.
5 Spoon into a greased lined 18 cm (7 inch) round cake tin and spread level.
Bake for 1½-2 hours. Test with a skewer to see if the cake is cooked through. Cool in the tin for 10 minutes, then turn out on to a wire rack.
6 Peel off the lining paper and store (when cold) in an airtight tin for a week to improve the flavour.

RECIPE COURTESY BILLINGTON'S

Not so cold now

Ruth with her doll's pram

Our country is getting warmer… I was born in 1931 and my father often had to dig his car out from our garage for weeks on end over the winter. We all had Wellingtons, boots, umbrellas and raincoats in the porch ready for going out.

My two older sisters asked for ice skates, skating skirt, hat, scarf and gloves and a sledge for Christmas presents.

When I was five, my mother took me to school up the hill on a sledge, then brought my scooter when collecting me, to come flying down the hill on top of the hard snow.

We all went skating on the park pond, and there would be lights on and music playing. My parents walked across the River Ouse at York when it froze – our grandchildren have never known such wonderful times.

Ruth Wright, York

✚YOUR GOOD HEALTH✚

Stay serene
Your first thought on waking can affect the whole day, says Tibetan medicine. So if you wake up feeling rushed, confused, or stressed, you're setting yourself up for difficulties. Try writing a list of thoughts on how you'd like your day to be – whether that's peaceful, loving or sociable – and keep it by your bed. First thing each morning, choose one thought from the list and focus on it for five minutes before you get up.

My Mum

Muriel and her mum, Lilian

There are so many things I remember about my wonderful Mum, Lilian…

The smell of fresh bread baked in different shapes for the harvest festival. Shining the grate for the range with black lead until you could see your face in it. Mum preparing a tray with a white traycloth and china cup saucer and milk jug for Mr Merryman, who was only the man that collected the grocery order, (I always thought he was an important man!)

We were always hard up, Mum brought up nine of us and I fear now she went short herself. I remember her sending us for 2d worth of neck-bones for the dog, which was Saturday night supper for us.

Mum would sit us on the doorstep with a greaseproof paper full of chips. All the kids would fetch their big potatoes for mum to cook them chips. It has been years now since she died but I miss her every day.

Muriel P Tutsell, Coventry

A RECIPE FOR YOU

Chinese Duck with Orange and Watercress
(Serves 4)

- 4 duck breast fillets
- 2 medium red onions, peeled and finely sliced
- 3 garlic cloves, peeled and finely sliced
- 300 ml ($\frac{1}{2}$ pt) orange juice
- 90 ml (6 tablespoons) hoisin sauce
- 2.5 cm (1 inch) piece root ginger, grated
- 1 x 350 g (12 oz) pack of mushroom stir-fry
- 1 85 g ($3\frac{1}{2}$ oz) bag watercress
- 30 ml (2 tablespoons) dark soy sauce mixed with 60 ml (4 tbsp) hot water
- **To serve:** Steamed rice and chopped salted peanuts

1 Score the skin of the duck in a criss-cross pattern to help the skin crisp up. Heat a wok to moderate heat, put the duck breasts in skin-side down. Cook for 8 minutes until skin is golden brown. Spoon off excess fat as it runs out and reserve. Turn the duck over and cook for a further 2 minutes. Transfer duck to a plate and leave to rest.

2 Wipe out the wok and add 30 ml (2 tablespoons) of the reserved duck fat. When it's hot, add the onion and garlic and stir-fry for 2-3 minutes until it caramelises. Add the orange juice and hoisin sauce, bring to the boil and cook for 30 seconds. Then add the duck, turn to a simmer and cook for 2 minutes. Transfer the duck and cooking liquid to a warm bowl and set aside.

3 Wipe the wok out, add another teaspoon of oil, and when hot add the ginger and mushroom stir-fry, watercress and soy sauce mixed with the water; stir-fry for 1 minute.

- **To serve:** Cut each duck breast vertically into three slices. Divide the rice between four serving plates, top with the vegetables, sliced duck and sauce. Sprinkle over the peanuts and serve.

RECIPE COURTESY THE FRESH CUT STIR FRY ALLIANCE

Plant of the week

A plant with the name naked ladies may entice you to grow it without even knowing what it is! However, it's well worth it and is so called because the flowers appear in the autumn well before their leaves – these don't emerge until the spring. The corms of Colchicum autumnale will even dry on a windowsill. Most varieties have flowers in shades of pink, peach or cerise. Outside, plant the corms in groups of three, about 15cm (6in) deep in well-drained soil that's enriched with compost.

● **Tip** – Never remove the leaves in late spring because the corms rely on these to replenish their reserves.

TOP TIP

If you've got a computer, type out people's addresses ready to put on labels for Christmas cards.

✚YOUR GOOD HEALTH✚

Save your skin

If you're prone to eczema, bitter winter weather and central heating can be bad news as they dehydrate your skin. Evening primrose oil helps soothe inflammation – take 1-4g daily – and zinc encourages skin healing, so take 30mg daily. For instant relief, try a homemade healing mask made with 2 tsp gram flour (from health food stores), 2 tsp almond oil and ¼ tsp of salt, then apply to the affected area and leave for 10 minutes.

And another thing...

Don't use flash if you're taking photos through a window, as the flash will reflect off the glass.

Memories of my daughter

Jeannie and her daughter

I wrote this verse many years after the birth of my daughter but now in my 80s, I can still remember the wonderful experience of her delivery on that stormy night in Cambridge.

New life
*Readied for birth, in gown
That rubs my elbows as I move.
Watching the shower's first drops
Stroking the window of this quiet room.
Peaceful nurse voices
Here for my comfort
Doing things they must, unobtrusive; kind.*

*Drowsy, waking to effort and drowse again
At rhythm with the lulls
And risings of the storm.
"Stay with me, healing rain,
Until my child is born."*

*Doctors, noting the progress
Of this miracle of birth.
The world encapsuled now
In this small room.
Bound by the blowing trees
And lashing rain – until
Over the loudest thunder roll,
My baby cries!*

Etiquette for Everybody
– 1920s' style –

On pointing...
'It is not polite to point at things; however, there are ways of pointing at things which are not objectionable.'

A treasured memento

Der-Der the rabbit, drawn by Priscilla's mother

Over the years I've collected mementos, a model, metal black and white Friesian cow from the farmyard set my parents gave me during the Second World War. I've an enamelled brooch of two Dutch children playing on a see-saw, a yellow nylon scarf that Grandma brought me from Folkestone in the 1950s.

But my most treasured memento is Der-Der, a Merrythought of Ironbridge toy, a gift from my great Aunt Olga when I was born in 1936. Der-Der kept me reassured during the war, when I slept in the shelter.

He went to school and barely left my side. One night, in 1941 in the shelter, my Mother drew his picture. He became shabby, so Mother covered him in an old skirt but his pink eyes shone still.

In May 1975 he stayed at home wearing a special bow for the day when Bob and I married.

Priscilla O'Dell, Hampton, Middx

And another thing...

The recipe for HP Sauce was created in Nottingham by a grocer called F G Garton. When he heard that it was being used in the Houses of Parliament, he decided to call it HP Sauce.

✚YOUR GOOD HEALTH✚

Go for yoghurt
People who eat a bowl of plain live yoghurt each day have 25 per cent fewer colds than non-yoghurt eaters. Scientists think that's because it's high in friendly lactobacillus and bifida bacteria, which help fight off germs. So spoon it over muesli, porridge and fruit to boost your immunity to those winter coughs and sneezes

A RECIPE FOR YOU

Spiced Pears
(Makes 900 g/2 lb)

- 900 g (2 lb) firm dessert pears
- 2 tbsp lemon juice
- 300 ml (approx $\frac{1}{2}$ pt) cider vinegar
- 150 ml ($\frac{1}{4}$ pt) apple juice
- 450 g (1 lb) granulated sugar
- 1 cinnamon stick, broken in half
- 12 cloves
- Small piece root ginger, roughly chopped

1 Peel, core and quarter the pears. Place in a pan with the lemon juice and cover with boiling water. Cook gently for about 15 minutes or until almost tender then drain.
2 Place the cider vinegar, apple juice, and 300 ml ($\frac{1}{2}$ pt) water with the granulated sugar, cinnamon sticks, cloves and ginger and heat gently, stirring frequently until the sugar has melted. Bring to the boil – boil vigorously for 5 minutes.
3 Add the drained pears and cook gently for 10 minutes. Remove from the heat and drain, reserving the spiced syrup. Pack the pears in sterilised warm jars.
4 Bring the spiced syrup to the boil, then carefully pour over the pears, seal with vinegar-proof lids and leave for at least 2 weeks to allow the pears to mature. Serve with either cold or roast meats. RECIPE COURTESY TATE & LYLE

An eventful journey

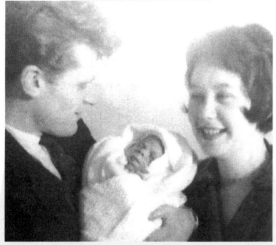

Frank, Jill and baby Karen in 1962

It all started on December 21st 1961, the day before my eldest daughter was born. We lived in Germany, as my husband Frank was a soldier. Snow was thick and it was 20 miles to the hospital – Karen was born six hours after arriving, and Frank had just a quick glance at her before returning to camp, as all transport was grounded.

Five weeks later, Frank was sent to the UK on a course and I travelled by plane two days earlier. My transport didn't turn up, so a friend offered to take me, but I missed the plane because his car broke down. I sent a message to Mum, who was waiting in London and when I arrived with baby daughter, carrycot and three large suitcases, there was no sign of her.

With the help of a good Samaritan, I caught the train to Carmarthen, but this country had also been hit by snow, so I was on the train for 14 hours! But the guard kept my flask topped up with hot water for Karen's bottles.

At Carmarthen, it still took me ages to get home to my village of Pendine because the snow was too deep to go anywhere, and I had to go on to St Clears. But transport arrived eventually, in the form of a three-ton Army truck, and Dad was at the gate to meet me. Some time later, Mum managed to get home (another difficult journey for her) and she saw her new granddaughter at last!

Jill Millward, Carmarthen

Plant of the week

Arum italicum is commonly called lords and ladies and the variety 'Marmoratum' is particularly attractive with large, arrow-shaped, glossy green leaves heavily marbled with cream. In spring it produces pale green spathes and these are followed during autumn by a display of vivid red berries. The plants thrive in the moist shade beneath trees and large clumps can be divided during May H30cm (1ft).

● **Tip** – Remove the outer pulp from the berries before you sow the seeds.

Etiquette for Everybody
– 1920s' style –

On shopping...
'Never purchase articles of which you have no real need. They will be dear at any price.'

TOP TIP

Adding a small amount of chopped fresh mint to soups will enhance the flavour enormously.

Wartime memories

With her husband Arthur away in the RAF, Mrs Millicent Shovelton of Ferndown in Dorset found herself alone, but busy

Millicent and husband Arthur

I gardened, grew vegetables and looked after the house. I shared the seeds with a friend who lived down the lane. Nothing was wasted. The egg ration was less than one per week and fresh milk was limited to two pints a week but we made nutritious meals. The vegetables I grew helped. I grew lots of potatoes. I bottled the fruit and made jam, but saving the sugar needed was difficult. Sometimes I used golden syrup as a sweetener.

From two to five on Tuesday afternoons I went to Mrs Tromans who used her large house for sewing. We had Singer sewing machines on which we made pyjamas and other garments for military hospitals. The materials and instructions were sent by the Ministry of Defence. We were also given wool in khaki, navy and airforce blue to knit gloves, socks and balaclavas at home.

I joined the WVS; part of our work was to offer our homes to one of the WAAFs who manned the nearby barrage balloon. Mine came on Wednesday afternoons to bath, wash her hair, write letters home. On some weekends, my WVS duties involved working at the British restaurant which provided reasonably priced meals for factory workers as well as service men and women.

On some Mondays, I helped at the Services Club, nine miles away in Birmingham, where I had a rota of jobs… making up beds, kitchen work, and serving the service men and women who stayed there.

I didn't always feel brave. Lovely autumn colours made me feel sad, as did music with special memories. I remember one winter's day when Bing Crosby singing I'm Dreaming of a White Christmas reduced me to tears, and I wept.

♻ Keen to be green / Everyday ways to save the plane

- Look for food with low air mileage instead of produce that has been air freighted thousands of miles for sale in supermarkets.

- Encourage any young mums you know to use cloth nappies instead of disposable ones – and give them the benefit of your heard-earned experience by showing them the different ways of folding for boy and girl babies!

- Instead of throwing away broken household items such as toasters or transistor radios, sell them cheaply at a garage or car boot sale to people who can make use of the spare parts.

- Pool DIY and garden tools with friends and family – it makes sense to share ones that are only occasionally needed.

- Instead of buying DVDs or videos that you will only watch once, it is better to hire them from a shop or your local library.

- Pretty greetings cards can be put to good use by using the front panel as a postcard.

- Plastic bottles make good containers for small items such as screws; cut three sides down to the same height, leaving the fourth side longer so that it can be nailed to the wall of the shed.

In the garden

- Put wet autumn leaves in a large plastic rubbish bag, tie some string round the neck then pierce some holes in it. Leave it for a year before using the broken down leafmould on your vegetable patch or flower beds.

- Cut up old tights and stockings to make plant ties.

- Broken crockery can be used for drainage at the bottom of pots.

Tell us about your best day of 2005!

Here we are at the start of 2006 and, judging by your kind letters, you've really enjoyed spending the year with the 2005 **Yours** Year Book.

We'd like to hear from you again if you had a day to remember in 2005. Perhaps you did something unusual for charity, perhaps you met an old friend after many years apart, or received a wonderful surprise.

Whatever your special day of 2005 was, we'd like you to tell us about it in no more than 350 words, and please try to send a photograph or two to accompany it – both of the special event and one of you as author. We'll keep the photos safe and return them in due course, but it will take a while.

We do hope you'll enter because the Best Day of 2004 competition entries we received were wonderful, and it was hard to choose the winner.

Send your entries to the address given on this page, by Tuesday, February 28, 2006.

And there's a great prize for the best entry!

The winner will receive £300 worth of travel vouchers to go towards a Travelscope holiday of their choice (subject to availability).

Tour operator Travelscope is dedicated to offering the most exciting and varied programme of holidays for **Yours** readers, ranging from UK and European breaks, to long haul flight holidays and ocean cruises.

Their award-winning selection of flight holidays promises not to disappoint with destinations such as Eygpt and Jordan, Hollywood, Vegas and the Grand Canyon, New York City Break, New Zealand, South Africa, Brazil and the Best of Italy and the Amalfi Coast.

Or why not go on a delightful River Cruise holiday on some of the most famous waterways in Europe? See Switzerland, Holland, Germany and France from a new perspective, and with many excellent facilities and a friendly crew, it will be a holiday to remember.

An Ocean Cruise allows you to escape the hustle and bustle of everyday life and relax as your own floating hotel brings the world to your window. Enjoy top class facilities on board Travelscope's 3 and 4 star cruise vessels to destinations such as St Petersburg, the Norwegian Fjords, Greenland, Iceland and further afield to New York, the Rio Carnival or why not travel the globe with our 93 day Round the World Cruise?

To order your free brochure today call 0870 770 5010 and quote reference YRA - you won't be disappointed!

● **Please send your Best Day of 2005 competition entries to Yours, Bretton Court, Bretton, Peterborough PE3 8DZ, marking your envelope Best Day of 2005. Usual Yours competition rules apply. Good luck!**

Henry goes shopping

by Beryl Lomas

Henry has a surprise when he takes a little rest from the pressures of Christmas shopping

Joan watched with amused exasperation as Henry stuck his head under the tap in a vain attempt to get his parting straight. They were going Christmas shopping and, true to form, Henry wore his frayed shirt with a clashing tie and what looked like his gardening trousers.

She remembered when she had first introduced Henry to her father. "You'll never do anything with him," he said as he surveyed the young man's ill-fitting suit and scuffed shoes. And he had been proved right. More than 50 years later, Henry still preferred his collection of moth-eaten shirts and baggy cardigans to any new clothes.

"Shall I bring that blue jacket down – the one you haven't worn yet?"

"No, this'll do," he replied, pulling on his brown corduroy jacket with the greasy mark on the sleeve. "I want to feel comfortable if we're wandering about all day."

"Shall I put you down for a haircut before Christmas?" Joan enquired, trying to sound casual. He looked at her in surprise. "It's not that long since you cut it last time," he said as he added a dab of Brylcreem and patted the final strand into place.

Any further debate about Henry's appearance was silenced by the sound of a car horn.

"Here's Helen!" Joan said, waving to her daughter from the window.

Henry opened the door to find Helen hidden

Henry heard the familiar tune of Away in a Manger

behind a pile of carrier bags and mysterious parcels. "Mum said it was okay to hide the kids' pressies here," she said, dropping one of them on his foot as she entered the hall. Henry helped her put them in the cupboard under the stairs.

"What's that delicious smell?" Helen asked sniffing the air.

"Your mother's dreaded mince pies," joked Henry. "I've thrown some out for the birds but they won't go near them."

"Cheeky beggar!" Joan shouted from the kitchen. "I heard that!" But she was chuckling. She couldn't have picked a better husband and she knew it. She told him often enough and his invariable response was: "You won't get round me like that you know; I'm not having my hair cut."

"Are you ready, then?" said Helen, rattling her car keys as Henry put on his overcoat. Joan sighed at its shabby state but thought that at least it covered the stain on his jacket sleeve.

As they parked in the multi-storey car park, Henry heard the familiar tune of Away in a Manger. "I bet that's the Sally Army," he said, clambering out of the car and leaning over the balcony.

The precinct was ablaze with colour. There were carousels for the children and a man in a striped apron was making up bags of hot chestnuts. A giant Christmas tree took centre stage, festooned in red, gold and white lights. The Salvation Army brass band struck up the first mellow chords of Silent Night and Henry smiled as

Joan cleared her throat ready to sing along.

"You get a smashing view from up here," he said. "Look at that sky over the hills." He pointed to where the horizon was pale grey, blue and pink. Sure enough, snow clouds were heading their way.

"We'd better get cracking," said Helen, "we don't want to get caught up in a snowstorm. What do we need first?"

"Your dad's present," said Joan, linking arms with Henry. He couldn't decide between a chess set or new garden shears so they wandered in and out of various shops in case he saw something else he fancied.

Joan and Helen made a couple of sneaky diversions into clothes shops which Henry studiously avoided.

He eventually settled on a nice pair of shears. He was delighted with them and kept diving in the carrier bag to inspect the box.

"That leaves only two more presents to buy," said Helen. Henry was getting a bit footsore and spotted a plastic chair outside a café. "I'll park myself here," he said, settling down comfortably on the seat. Soon he began to doze off. He woke

with a start as a man leant over him, saying, "Merry Christmas!"

"Thank you," Henry responded, rubbing his eyes. He didn't recognise the man and struggled to see who it was as he disappeared round the corner. Probably someone he used to work with, he reflected. Quite soon, he nodded off again, dreaming that other passers-by also paused to wish him the season's greetings.

He was woken by Joan tapping him on the shoulder. He yawned and looked round, trying to get his bearings. Helen was laughing and Joan clearly didn't know whether to laugh or cry. His hat, which he'd placed on his knees, was heavy with coins dropped in by passing shoppers.

"There's over fifteen pounds in here!" Helen counted.

Henry was torn between amusement and indignation. Then he announced: "Well, there's only one thing for it, I'm off to buy a new winter coat and hat!"

Joan and Helen were speechless and set off in disbelieving pursuit as he headed towards the nearest department store. Passing the Salvation Army band, Henry pressed his battered hat and its contents into the hands of a grateful horn player. The strains of God Rest Ye Merry Gentlemen followed him as he pulled the smartest tweed overcoat he could find from the rail and tried it on.

He didn't recognise the man and struggled to see who it was...

Friday

1

World Aids Day

Saturday

2

Sunday

3

Monday

4

Tuesday

5

Wednesday

6

Yours December 6 issue on sale

Thursday

7

Friday

8

Saturday

9

Sunday

10

Monday

11

Tuesday

12

Wednesday

13

Thursday

14

Friday

15

Saturday

16

Sunday

17

Monday

18

Tuesday

19

Wednesday

20

Thursday

21

Friday

22

Saturday

23

Sunday

24

Monday

25   Christmas Day

Tuesday

26   Boxing Day

Wednesday

27

Thursday

28

Friday

29

Saturday

30

Sunday

31

Flavour of the month

The weeks leading up to Christmas simply fly by with so much to do in readiness for the festivities. There are presents to buy and wrap, menus to plan and decorations to put up. In the midst of all the hustle and bustle, spare a thought for those who are likely to be alone at this special time of the year and, if you know such a person, why not invite them to join your family celebrations?

Every year the complaint is heard of how commercial Christmas has become but it is possible to capture the true spirit of the season without spending more than we can really afford. If you have time, make your own greetings cards, and use last year's to cut up for use as gift tags. Instead of an expensive fir tree,

paint a few interestingly shaped branches white and decorate them with coloured baubles or ribbon tied in bows .

Being creative is fun for all the family. Given a little encouragement, children love to make their own contribution by cutting out coloured paper chains or picking ivy to twist into a simple wreath for the front door.

December 21, St Thomas's Day, is the shortest day of the year. In some parts of the country, broad beans were planted on this day. And if you want to learn what sort of weather is in store over the next few months, this is the day to know your onions! Old country lore has it that if their skins are thin, the winter will be mild, but thick skins foretell severe weather conditions.

My Mum

I'd been accepted to train as an SRN in 1956 but because I wasn't 18, I had to start as a pre-nursing student for nine months. This being the first time away from home, my Mother said she'd make the long journey with me.

When I reported to Matron she instructed me to go to the Nurses' Hostel, about five minutes' walk from the hospital. My Mother came with me, and when we arrived at the gate I started to cry when I had to say goodbye.

My first Christmas away, I used to telephone from the kiosk near my home as I wasn't allowed to use the telephone in the hostel. I was chatting away until the pips went; I started crying and the operator said, "Oh, go on – have a few more minutes."

I spent many more Christmases away from home but I shall always remember that first one. I became an SRN on April 4, 1960 and I retired when I was 60 years old.

Mrs Annette L Madden, Torfaen

Above: SRN Annette in 1960
Below: Annette's mum in 1986, on her 73rd birthday

Etiquette for Everybody
– 1920s' style –

On letter writing…
'Avoid gushing in letters, and think twice before you put in black and white things which may lead to trouble.'

And another thing...

Have you noticed that when your arms are filled with Christmas parcels, the sign on the shop door always says, 'Pull'?

✚YOUR GOOD HEALTH✚

Boost blood flow

Feeling the cold? If you have bad circulation or Raynaud's Syndrome, which stops enough blood getting to your extremities, leading to numbness and tingling, the colder months can be miserable. The herb ginkgo biloba helps improve blood flow – take 120mg daily, but speak to your doctor first if you're on prescription medication.

My Prayer

If only…
We could have a Christmas with happiness guaranteed
To every human being, irrespective of colour or creed
Where no one would be lonely, the homeless would have a bed
And every living child would be loved, and warm and fed
All nations would be reconciled, all voices joined together
To sing of love and understanding and peace that lasts forever.
Mrs Hilda M Yates, Hoghton, Preston

Plant of the week

It may seem odd to include a deciduous grass such as Stipa tenuissima at the end of the year, but this little character has attractive wispy seedheads above its bronzing leaves and remains delightfully strokeable well into winter. Ideal in borders and containers, it looks best when planted with larger members of its family including S arundinacea and S gigantea which are similar in habit. Here it's with cyclamen and heathers. H60cm (2ft).

● **Tip** – Plant it where you can enjoy it billowing in the slightest breeze.

A treasured memento

Maureen smiling for the camera

From the age of 16 until I was 45 years, my Dad always gave me a box of Cadbury's chocolates, gloves or stockings, and a diary for Christmas, as well as my 'main present'.

In 1981, however, I received a cameo scarf clip and a book of verse by Patience Strong. Four months later he died, having first asked me to read particular verses from the book. They certainly helped me to come to terms with his death, and the scarf clip is my most treasured possession.

Maureen Knighton, Kettering

A RECIPE FOR YOU

Rack of Lamb with a Herb Crust and Marsala and Redcurrant Sauce
(Serves 4)

● 2 lean racks of lamb

For the Herb Crust
● 90 ml (6 tablespoons) freshly chopped parsley, chives or thyme leaves
● 50 g (2 oz) butter, melted
● 100 g (4 oz) fresh breadcrumbs
● Zest of 1 lemon
● Salt and freshly milled black pepper
● 1-2 tsps English mustard

For the sauce
● 25 g (1 oz) butter
● 1 tablespoon plain flour
● 125 ml (4 fl oz) Marsala or pale sherry
● 250 ml (9 fl oz) hot, good lamb or chicken stock
● 2-3 teaspoons redcurrant jelly

1 Preheat the oven to 180-190°C, 350-375°F, Gas Mark 4-5.
2 Prepare the herb crust: Place all the ingredients except the mustard into a food processor and blend until combined.
3 Place the racks of lamb, fat side up, on a chopping board, and brush the mustard over to apply a good coating.
4 Press a generous handful of the herb crust over the racks. Transfer to a medium-sized roasting tin and roast for 25 minutes per 450 g (1 lb) plus 25 minutes. Cover the bones with foil if browning too quickly.
5 To make the gravy, heat the butter in a saucepan, sprinkle over the flour and stir well with a small whisk or spoon. Add the Marsala or sherry, stir and bring to the boil and reduce the liquid to half the quantity. Stir in the stock and the redcurrant jelly. Simmer for 2-3 minutes until well-flavoured gravy develops. Season to taste.
6 Slice the racks and serve 2-3 cutlets per person with baby new potatoes and seasonal green beans.

RECIPE COURTESY OF QUALITY STANDARD BEEF AND LAMB

December 4-10

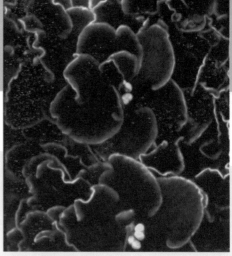

And another thing...

In the churchyard at Lyndhurst in Hampshire lies Mrs Reginald Hargreaves, better known as Alice Liddell, the inspiration for Lewis Carroll's Alice in Wonderland

✚YOUR GOOD HEALTH✚

Spice it up

Warming spices are great for adding a zing to your cooking and helping you feel comforted on chilly days. But they're also good news for your health – ginger boosts the circulation and immune system, chillies aid digestion, and turmeric could help prevent dementia, so sprinkle them all into your cooking. For winter aches and pains, add a spoonful each of sugar and turmeric to a glass of lime juice, and drink.

Plant of the week

African violets have long been one of our favourite houseplants – they're long flowering, you can buy them in flower all year round, they come in a wide range of colours and they're simple to look after. Discovered by Baron St Paul Illaire in the 1800s, hence their common name of Saint Paulias, they thrive in moist soil in bright but not direct sunlight. Avoid getting the leaves wet. H 15cm (6in).
● **Tip** – Always water into the saucer the pot is sitting in.

A treasured memento

The five Dionne quin dolls

It was 1934 and in Canada five little girls had been born to Elzire Dionne, in Corbeil, Ontario…

In the 1930s, if your Dad was out of work over Christmas, the teacher would say, 'Put your hand up', for a free Christmas treat. (My dear Dad worked hard to feed five mouths but he was sometimes laid off.) I put up my hand, and went off to my treat at the local cinema, to see a film, a stage show and receive a surprise bag of goodies as I left.

The Mayor of Islington was on stage with a big mirror and said, whoever this shines on must come up and receive a big prize. And it shone on me! The mayor gave me a long brown box…

Opening the box at home, I found five little 'Dionne quin' dolls in a cot, lying on a pink blanket, with their names – Marie, Cicile, Emilie, Annette and Yvonne – at the bottom of the cot. I very seldom played with them but just sat them up in their cot to look at.

Etiquette for Everybody
– 1920s' style –

On dining…
'Never accept a second helping of anything if by so doing you will retard the progress of the party. Soup and fish are never taken in duplicate. If certain foods do not suit you, reject them without commenting on the sufferings which they inflict on your digestion.'

TOP TIP

When a tube of toothpaste is nearly empty, use a good strong elastic band around the base to push the remainder up towards the top. It works well.
Lena Jones, Flint, Clwyd

A RECIPE FOR YOU

Fruity Dark Chocolate Christmas Cake

- 175 g (6 oz) good quality plain chocolate – at least 60 per cent cocoa solids
- 110 g (4 oz) unsalted butter
- 150 g (5 oz) molasses sugar
- 4 large eggs, beaten
- 150 g (5 oz) self-raising flour
- 2 tablespoons cocoa powder
- 75 g (3 oz) ground almonds
- 5 tablespoons dark beer or stout
- 2 teaspoons ground cinnamon
- 1/2 teaspoon ground mixed spice
- Grating of nutmeg
- 100 g (4 oz) prunes, pitted
- 100 g (4 oz) raisins
- 175 g (6 oz) glacé cherries
- 100 g (4 oz) currants
- 100 g (4 oz) walnuts, roughly chopped
- 100 g (4 oz) candied peel, chopped

1 Melt the chocolate in a bowl over a pan of simmering water. Remove from pan and cool slightly.
2 Meanwhile cream the butter and molasses sugar in a mixing bowl until light, then whisk in the melted chocolate. Gradually add the beaten eggs, whisking well.
3 Sift in the flour and cocoa, and gently fold into the mixture. Fold in the ground almonds, beer and spices, followed by the fruits and walnuts.
4 Spoon into a deep 23 cm (9 in) round cake tin lined with non-stick baking paper to come above the edges of the tin.
5 Level the top and cook for 1 hour at 170 °C, 325°F, Gas Mark 3, then reduce to 140°C, 275°F, Gas Mark 1 for 1-1½ hours until a skewer comes out clean. Cool in the tin for 15 minutes then place on a wire rack.
6 Wrap well when cold and store in a cool place until ready to ice.

Golden Frosting
- 450g/1 lb golden granulated sugar
- 150 ml/5 fl oz water
- pinch of cream of tartar
- 2 egg whites

1 Heat the sugar and water in a heavy-based pan over a low heat until sugar has dissolved. Add the cream of tartar. Bring to the boil, then boil steadily for 3 minutes at 115°C (240°F) on a sugar thermometer.
2 Whisk the egg whites until very stiff. Pour the hot syrup in a thin stream onto the egg whites, whisking constantly. Continue whisking until the mixture is thick enough to stand in peaks.
3 Quickly spread over the cake.   RECIPE COURTESY BILLINGTON'S

An unforeseen driving test

Penny, aged 18, took to driving early

I'd put up my age by one year and joined the ATS as a driver in 1941, passing my test a week or so before I was 17.

Where I was billeted, I had to take my car down a steep hill to our garages and saw my Sergeant, and I thought, 'I'm driving too fast, again.'

It was my first experience of driving in snow and I braked, only to broadside down the hill. When I stopped, Sergeant congratulated me on how I'd handled the car. I never knew if she guessed why I'd skidded!

Penny Dickson, Chorleywood, Herts

A RECIPE FOR YOU
Spiced Cherry and Red Wine Soup

- 675 g (approx 1½ lb sweet red and black cherries)
- ½ litre (18 fl oz) fruity red wine
- 75 g-110 g (3-4 oz) light muscovado sugar (depending on the sweetness of the cherries)
- Grated zest and juice of 1 small lemon
- 1 cinnamon stick
- ¼ teaspoon ground cloves (optional)
- Splash of kirsch (optional)

1 Stone the cherries and reserve any juice.
2 Heat the wine, sugar, lemon zest and spices (if using) in a pan until boiling, then cover and leave to stand for at least 2 hours.
3 Strain into a clean pan and add the cherries and reserved juice. Simmer gently for about 15 minutes or until the cherries are tender.
4 Purée the mixture with a hand-held blender or in a food processor until smooth. Return to the pan.
5 Taste and add a squeeze or two of lemon juice to sharpen the flavour, if necessary. Add a dash of kirsch if liked. This can be served either hot as a starter or cold as a dessert, with a dollop of whipped cream. Omit the cinnamon and cloves if you don't want a spicy flavour.

RECIPE COURTESY BILLINGTON'S

Maureen at her daughter's wedding, with her mother, in August 2004

My Mum

My Mother never had idle hands. We always had hand knitted garments as far back as I can remember. My sisters and I all wore dresses knitted in 'Robin Perle' as children, when these were extremely fashionable. When she did have the opportunity to sit down in the evening once the little ones were settled, she knitted as she listened to the radio.

Mum managed to find time to cook for all of us, making jams, cakes, and what seemed like mountains of food, for a family of nine. As we grew up we took over some of the chores and all had our separate duties, but she continued to cook delicious food and knit for us. One Christmas we four girls each had a doll all dressed from head to toe in knitted clothes.

Until the age of 85 she still knitted for her great grandchildren, for a local premature baby unit, crocheted shawls for each new baby born to friends, neighbours or family, went to crochet classes, and made patchwork cushions.

Mum died in November 2004, aged 86, and is much missed but I 'm sure that when St Peter met her at the pearly gates she said: "I'll just have to finish this row."

Mrs Maureen Santi, Hailsham

✚YOUR GOOD HEALTH✚

Clear your lungs

Smokey dinner parties can leave your chest feeling congested. A steam inhalation with detoxifying essential oils can help blitz it, as the steam carries the healing properties of the oil directly to your lungs. Add three to four drops of cleansing eucalyptus essential oil to a bowl of steaming water, then bend over it, head covered, for five minutes, inhaling deeply. Avoid if you have asthma.

Plant of the week

Sedges are great evergreen plants because they immediately add structure to a planting scheme, yet are simple to grow and are attractive all year round. Carex 'Silver Sceptre' is elegant with green leaves with a crisp white margin. Slightly spreading, it thrives in moist soil in sun or partial shade. H30cm (1ft)

● **Tip** – It looks lovely cascading at the edge of a water feature.

And another thing...

'Love is like the measles; we all have to go through it.'　　*Jerome K Jerome*

A treasured memento

The Christmas shopping was done, with wrapping paper and gift tags lying on the table. I was banished to the kitchen while my husband supervised the wrapping of presents for 'Mum'. Our two daughters were old enough to keep a secret – not so our four-year-old son. He couldn't wait to tell me what was in the parcel. A couple of days passed, and he could keep it to himself no longer. Whispering loudly in my ear, he announced, 'It's a pen, Mum, for you to write letters.'

This was back in Christmas 1973 and was to be our most memorable one as our young son was to be taken from us a year later.

Above: Helen and grandson, Anthony, on the lawn.
Left: Helen today

He died from cancer at the age of five.

My pen? It's still in use, and brings back memories of our special Christmas.

There's little doubt, of all the pleasures we can dream of, children bring the most of all and I am happy to say we now have four grandchildren.

　Mrs Helen Gibb, Midlothian

Etiquette for Everybody
– 1920s' style –

On home conduct...
'Families where no servant is kept are the most liable to degenerate in manners, because there is no outsider to act as a check to thoughtless and slovenly habits.'

TOP TIP

If you sleep in a double bed on your own, put a pillow or better still, a bolster on the other side of the bed close to you. It's really cosy during the cold winter nights.

　Mrs I Pearson, Birmingham

A treasured memento

Left: Panto programme with Stanley Baxter on the cover. Below Nancy and granddaughter Abigail, when she was 12.

I have a theatre programme of a pantomime starring Stanley Baxter at The King's Theatre, Glasgow which is a very special memento to me.

My husband and I often spent the Christmas holidays in Scotland where our son lived and worked then. We had two lovely grandchildren, Abigial and Jaimie, and one Christmas we decided to go to the pantomime. Abi had never been to a panto, so there was great excitement! Of course, the 'look behind you' routine was full of joyful shouts, the colourful stage clothes, and dear Mother Goose herself, Stanley Baxter, made everyone cry with laughter. Abi felt the true magic of the traditional, and well-loved, glorious pantomimes of Christmas times.

Abi, at 27 years of age, still doesn't know that I carefully saved this colourful memento programme… she will eventually!

Mrs Nancy Lowther, Cliftonville, Kent

✚YOUR GOOD HEALTH✚

Going bananas

Most of us overdo the booze at this time of year. If you're hungover, forget the fry-ups – you may crave fatty foods but they'll just put more strain on your liver. Your best bet is the humble banana. It's rich in potassium, the mineral that helps balance body fluids, and magnesium, to help correct blood sugar levels. Plus it contains vitamin C, another vital post-drinking nutrient!

A RECIPE FOR YOU

Pistachio, Praline and Chocolate Mousse
(Serves 4)

- 25 g (1 oz) granulated cane sugar
- 1 tablespoon unsalted, shelled pistachios, chopped
- 75 g (3 oz) white chocolate
- 150 ml (¼ pt) 'light' double cream alternative*
- 1 medium egg white

1 Place the granulated cane sugar in a heavy-based small pan and cook over a gentle heat for 1-2 mins, shake the pan occasionally until all the sugar has melted, then caramelised.
2 Stir in the pistachios and remove from the heat. Carefully pour the caramel mixture on to an oiled baking sheet and leave until cold. Smash the praline with a rolling pin, reserving a few pieces for decoration, then finely crush the remainder.
3 Melt the chocolate in a bowl placed over a pan of hot water. Whisk the egg white and light double cream, in separate bowls, until they form soft peaks. Fold into the chocolate with the crushed praline.
4 Divide between four dessert glasses and top with the reserved praline shards.
- Cartons of reduced fat cream alternative are available from most supermarkets in double, single and light varieties. The 'light double' works well in this recipe.

RECIPE COURTESY TATE & LYLE

Young love

Left: Eileen and Jim on their wedding day in 1966
Above: Eileen and Jim on holiday in 2000

I met Jim in 1957, when were both nine years old, and we've now been married 38 years.

Jim tells me that he always knew he wanted to marry me and I still fall for his smooth talk, but I knew he was special when, at the age of 12, I was getting over the flu and my mother had set up a bed for me in the little-used living room. She'd been busy that day and the room was cold and looked as miserable as I felt, so when Jim came round to see how I was, she allowed him in to talk to me.

Within minutes, he'd talked her into letting him light a fire, then he plumped up my pillows and made me a cup of Bovril. As I sat with my comforting drink and let the crackling fire cheer me, I revised my views of Jimmy O'Shea and within a few weeks I'd promised to marry him when he gave me a highly ornate gold and ruby ring from Woolworth's.

We married on New Year's Eve in 1966 and have two daughters – the pride of our lives – and five smashing grandchildren.

Eileen O'Shea, Ballymena, Co Antrim

And another thing...

'We're having the same old thing for Christmas this year... relatives'   *Mark Twain*

Plant of the week

Everyone likes to see berries at Christmas and there are several plants which put on a colourful show, such as Skimmia japonica reevesiana. A great border plant, it thrives in partial shade and can also be used in containers to create a warm welcome beside your front door. Once it has outgrown the container, plant it back in the garden. Most skimmias are dioecious, which means they have male and female flowers on different plants and both sexes must be planted to ensure fruiting.
● **Tip** – The subspecies reevesiana is an hermaphrodite and will produce berries if planted on its own. The berries last all autumn and winter.

TOP TIP

Fill hanging baskets with old cut up wool in the spring and birds will come and take it for nesting material.

My Mum

I have so many memories of my Mum. She was always full of fun and did mad things, which my brother and I loved.

One memory of her is of a Christmas when I was a child. My Mother was a midwife and always seemed to be on call on Christmas Day. We'd been playing charades and Mum was dressed up in trousers, bowler hat, droopy moustache and a blackened face, when she received a telephone call saying that a birth was imminent.

It sounded very urgent, my

Mother arrived at the patient's house still sporting everything, complete with blackened face and droopy moustache!

Mum always maintained that the very quick delivery was caused by the shock of seeing this 'moustached and black-faced man' heading for her bed with the obvious intention of delivering her baby!

Ms E Marcia Higgins,
Barrow-on-Soar

Left: Marcia's mum
Centre: Marcia today
Above: Marcia's mum – always full of fun – enjoying a swing, with Marcia pushing!

TOP TIP

Before you take your Christmas cards off to be recycled, choose some to cut up for labels for next Christmas's presents

A treasured memento

Just before New Year's Eve 1925, my Dad, Joe, returned from sea and bought my beloved mother, Lillah, a beautifully large wooden box which he had had made for her by his ship's carpenter. The initials 'L M' were inlaid in the lid.

It had beautiful, tiny, brass fittings and two minute drawers inside the box. There was also a secret spring which, when pressed, caused a little drawer to open, and underneath the drawer my dad had written:
'Heaps of love
From Joe to Lillah
New Year's Day 1925'

I now have the box – which is as beautiful now as the day it was made aboard a ship thousands of miles away – and will always treasure it.

Mrs Beryl Hewitson,
Henfield, West Sussex

Top: Beryl's late mother Lillah's box
Above: Lillah and Joe in 1927
Left: Beryl, by the sea

Plant of the week

One of the best houseplants at Christmas is the Indian azalea. It likes a light position, but not direct sunshine, so an east, west or north-facing windowsill is ideal. Increase the humidity by placing it on a tray of moist gravel and use lime-free water, such as fresh rainwater, to keep it moist. It is difficult to over-water Indian azaleas but they tend to drop their leaves and flowerbuds if allowed to dry out, so water it every other day to be on the safe side. Place the plants outside during the summer and bring in again as temperatures fall.

● **Tip** – if you haven't any rainwater, acidify your tap water by adding a teabag to it a day previously.

Etiquette for Everybody
– 1920s' style –

On conversation…
'The weather is a topic upon which we all rely at times. Always hit upon something else if possible. But never discuss your ailments

And another thing...

Dear Santa Claus
   Please can I have just one teddy bear for Christmas; nothing else, just a teddy bear.
   Love Sophia
   PS Please can teddy have a portable television to keep teddy amused when I'm at school.

A RECIPE FOR YOU
Roast Beef Topside
with Stilton and Hazelnut Stuffing
(Serves 4-6)

● 1.25 kg (2½ lbs) lean beef topside joint, rolled and tied
● Salt and fresh black pepper
● 25-50 g (1-2 oz) butter, softened
● 1-2 tablespoons freshly chopped parsley
● 6 tablespoons cranberry sauce
● 6 tablespoons port
● 1 tablespoon plain flour
● 300 ml (approx ½ pint) hot beef stock

For the Stilton and Hazelnut Stuffing
● 75 g (3 oz) fresh breadcrumbs
● 2 tablespoons fresh chopped chives
● 25 g (1 oz) hazelnuts, roughly chopped
● 25 g (1 oz) mushrooms, finely chopped
● 25 g-50 g (1-2 oz) Stilton, crumbled
● 1 medium egg, beaten

1 Season the topside joint.
2 Mix together the softened butter and parsley. Spread generously over the joint. Transfer to a metal rack, place in a roasting tin and cook – for rare, 20 minutes per 450 g (1 lb), plus 20 mins, for medium, 25 minutes per 450 g (1 lb, plus 25 minutes, and well done, 30 minutes per 450 g (1 lb) plus 30 minutes.
3 For the stuffing: Mix together breadcrumbs, chives, hazelnuts, mushrooms, Stilton and egg. Shape the mixture into 10-12 balls, place on to a non-stick baking sheet and cook during the last 15 minutes of the roasting time.
4 Mix together the cranberry sauce and the port. 20-30 minutes before the end of cooking, brush over the joint. Remove the joint from the oven, place on to a platter, wrap loosely in foil and set aside to rest. Reserve meat juices.
5 **To make the gravy:** Spoon off any excess fat from the roasting tin and discard. Place the roasting tin over a medium heat and sprinkle over the flour. Stir well, add a little stock and stir again. Add the remaining stock, and any meat juices from the platter and simmer for 8-10 minutes.

● This recipe contains nuts   RECIPE COURTESY QUALITY STANDARD BEEF AND LAMB

Wartime memories

Mr Brian Jones of Whitstable was aged just two and a half when the war started but he has not forgotten the drama of day-to-day life

Brian recalls wartime memories

We lived in Folkestone at the foot of the North Downs, an area known then as Hellfire Corner. Some of my most vivid memories are of British and German bombers that droned on day and night. If they were enemy planes, very noisy ack-ack guns tried to shoot them down. Later, when the Americans joined the war, there were enormous Flying Fortresses, glinting in the sun. Flying in formation, they were quite a sight.

We all had gas masks issued in case there was a gas attack and these were awful to wear. They were very tight and difficult to breathe in. In the first few years of the war, you had to carry them with you at all times.

We didn't have any sweets, chocolate or ice creams. I can remember buying Melloids which were little globules of liquorice. When the Americans came over, it was common practice for children to go up to a GI and ask: "Got any gum, chum?" then a strip of gum might be handed over and gratefully received. There was always enough food, although some of it was repetitive and boring – I didn't like powdered eggs or Spam. The rather monotonous meals included pease pudding which I have hated ever since. If my mother heard that any items normally in short supply were in the shops, she used to send me down to queue for her as it needed a lot of patience.

I grew excited at Christmas even though dinner usually consisted of an old hen that had given up laying and been killed for the festivities. It was rather tough. I always had a Rupert Bear annual and usually something like tin soldiers or farmyard animals.

♻ Keen to be green / Everyday ways to save the plane

Four ways to re-use plastic carrier bags:
● Scrunch them up around fragile items to be sent through the post.
● When going on holiday, use them to wrap round shoes in your suitcase and as a receptacle for dirty laundry.
● When walking the dog, take one to use as a poop-scoop.
● Take them back to the supermarket to be recycled.

● When a light bulb goes, replace it with a low energy one. The initial cost is higher but it pays off in the long run. See website www.lamprecycle.org for details of a group that re-uses light bulbs.

● When you have read your copy of **Yours**, pass it on, with other magazines, to dentists, doctors and hospitals to put in their waiting rooms. Residential homes are also glad to receive magazines.

● Instead of disposable goods, give your loved ones tickets for the theatre, cinema or concert as presents.

● Buy locally grown fruit and vegetables from your nearest farmers' market instead of the supermarket.

● Avoid buying expensively packaged sandwiches from shops by making your own – they will be fresher and taste better, too.

● Everyone has lists to make at Christmas, so save envelopes and any unused scraps of paper to write on. The oval piece of cardboard that has to be removed from the top of a box of tissues is ideal for longer lists.

In the garden
● Aluminium containers that have been used for cooking can be rinsed and saved for use as seed trays.

● Climate change means milder winters when weeds still go on growing; suppress them with layers of newspaper spread on the ground and covered with tree bark or gravel.

Holiday Heaven

Yours holidays

Get away from it all with one of our Round the World cruises

WORLD CRUISE 2007 (YRA/RTE)

Departing: October 12, 2007 from FALMOUTH

85 Days From: £2799 based on four sharing

Say goodbye to the cold bleak British winter and experience some of the world's greatest treasures including the ancient Pyramids of Giza, the Great Barrier Reef and the Panama Canal on board the excellent 4* Plus MV Athena. Spend Christmas in the sun-kissed Caribbean, before welcoming in the New Year admiring the spectacular fireworks display in Madeira. All from an unbelievable £2,799 per person!

Easy payment scheme available

Included...

✔ Complimentary coaching from selected pick up points or free car parking at Falmouth ✔ 84 nights' accommodation on board the 4* Plus MV Athena ✔ 24 ports of call including Barbados on Christmas Eve and Madeira on New Year's Eve ✔ Excellent on board facilities including swimming pool, fitness centre, cinema and casino ✔ Choice of cabins with full private facilities, air conditioning and TV ✔ Full board — breakfast, lunch, afternoon tea, dinner and midnight snacks ✔ Live entertainment each evening ✔ Exciting range of optional shore excursions available ✔ All Port Taxes included

24 PORTS OF CALL, including...
Gibraltar ★ Malta ★ Egypt ★ Oman ★ India ★ Sri Lanka ★ Thailand ★ Malaysia ★ Singapore ★ Bali ★ Australia ★ New Caledonia ★ Fiji ★ Niue ★ Cook Islands ★ Tahiti ★ Marquesas Islands ★ Ecuador ★ Transit Panama Canal ★ Aruba ★ St. Lucia ★ Barbados (Christmas Eve) ★ Madeira (New Year's Eve)

★ **Also available** ★

WORLD CRUISE 2008 (YRA/RTW)

Departing: January 4, 2008 from FALMOUTH

There are few experiences more aspirational than a world cruise, a sublime global voyage following in the footsteps of famous explorers and travellers throughout the ages. Leave the cold bleak British Winter behind and embark on a halcyon journey to a wonderful world of shimmering seas, glorious sunshine and sensational sunsets on board the 4* Plus MV Athena.

24 PORTS OF CALL (18 countries, 4 continents) including...
★ Azores ★ Antigua ★ Guadeloupe, French Caribbean ★ Dutch Caribbean ★ San Blas Islands, Panama ★ Equador ★ Marquesas Islands ★ Tahiti ★ French Polynesia ★ Tonga ★ Fiji ★ New Zealand ★ Australia ★ Tasmania ★ Mauritius ★ Réunion ★ South Africa ★ St Helena ★ Ascension Island ★ Cape Verde ★ Madeira

93 Days From: £2999 based on four sharing

★ **Book both world cruises for a 5% discount** ★

★ It couldn't be easier to book call now on 0870 770 5010

This holiday is operated by Travelscope Holidays Ltd ABTA V5060